The Sacred Spark

Exploring the Hidden Gifts of ADHD in Spiritual Leadership

Katharine L. Steele

Tehom Center Publishing is a 501(c)3 nonprofit publishing feminist and queer authors, with a commitment to elevate BIPOC writers. Its face and voice is Rev. Dr. Angela Yarber.

Paperback ISBN: 978-1-966655-41-1

Ebook ISBN: 978-1-966655-42-8

Contents

Introduction   13

1. A CALL TO CURIOSITY   21
Uncovering the intersection of clergywomen and ADHD

2. GENDER AND MINISTRY   39
Navigating the weight of an uneven pulpit

3. HIDDEN IN PLAIN SIGHT   47
The gendered presentation of ADHD in women and girls

4. PERSONAL NARRATIVE AS LIVED INQUIRY   57
Diagnosis, identity, and pastoral formation

5. REREADING BETHANY   65
Reimagination and neurodivergent possibility

6. MINISTRY IN THE MARGINS   75
Findings on ADHD and clergywomen's vocational realities

7. THE INTERSECTION OF ADHD AND MINISTRY   85
Toward a fuller understanding of VAST in clergywomen

8. TOWARD A FAITHFUL RESPONSE   97
Recommendations for supporting neurodivergent clergywomen

Conclusion   115

Bibliography   119

*To all the uniquely called, qualified and gifted clergywomen with ADHD:
I see you. You're amazing. Keep following God's call.*

Acknowledgements

"Deep gratitude" seems an insufficient phrase for the astounding amount of emotion I feel as I think back upon the many people and organizations that helped this project come to life. A factor here *could be* the emotional dysregulation I often experience, but I think it's more than that. Truly, without the following individuals and groups, this book would still be nothing more than a glimmer of a thought of an amorphous concept and nothing more.

To Janet and Edward Steele, my unendingly supportive parents who, despite my silly hope and misplaced expectations of the opposite, nudged me further into pursuing my Doctor of Ministry degree as opposed to talking me back from the metaphorical edge, and for their subsequent financial contributions to the endeavor.

To my colleague and friend, Rev. Robert English, who opened the door of possibility and the magnanimous community at Mt. Healthy UMC for their generous financial support of my education that saw me through to the finish line.

For my faculty advisor, Dr. Angela Yarber and professional mentor Dr. Valerie Schrader, I give thanks. Dr. Ang, you inspire me in more ways than I know how to count, thank you for your effervescent and infectious belief in a better world and the irresistible way you inspire the rest of us with unmitigated hope. Val, there are few gifts more precious on this earth than to realize that you have found an *anam cara* or "soul friend." You and the Red Tent ladies (Kirstin, Cat, and Jess) have buoyed me through so much for almost two decades. Thank you for taking this "side quest" with me in academia—it's been fun!

To my colleagues and student leaders at Wesley Campus Ministry at Miami University and Oxford UMC as well as my beloved students, thank you for all the ways you stepped up and assisted, planned, and collaborated to keep the ministry afloat during my most distractable days. Thank you for allowing me the time away to hyperfocus so I could complete the tasks of writing, editing and publishing. Your support, encouragement, and understanding were invaluable in those final weeks as the pressure mounted and the deadlines loomed.

My thanks to local indie bookstores and public libraries everywhere, but especially to Hidden Chapter Bookstore in Ft. Thomas, Kentucky, Roebling Books & Coffee in Newport, Kentucky, the Forest Park Library in Cincinnati, Ohio, King Library at Miami University in Oxford, Ohio, and the Bexley Public Library in Columbus, Ohio where much of what you are about to read was drafted, edited, highlighted, fretted over, and eventually compiled for submission. Long live libraries and third spaces where we can find and create the words we need to change the world! And thanks for copy editors everywhere, but especially the irreplaceable Tina Knaier, my first adopted older sister and biggest cheerleader; I stand in awe and give my humble thanks for your attention to detail and loving mark-ups.

To my oldest and longest friends as well as newer and deep enduring friends I made as an adult, thank you for keeping me in your circles. Truly, you have saved my life on more than one occasion, especially when the "bitch translator" who lives in my brain tries to tell me that I'm not worth anyone's friendship. To my Girl Scout sisters and YCWI colleagues who "get it." And especially to Miska, Alissa, Kara, Stephanie, and Sam, thank you for seeing me and loving me just as I am over all these years. Your abiding friendship through the years means more to me than I can ever hope to convey.

Thank you to everyone who supplied caffeine (Erin!), meals (Alan, Megan and fam), body-doubling time and accountability. To those who let me stay in their guest rooms (Marta, Joel and Wendy) or otherwise helped fund writing retreats for deep focus. For my editors and beta readers and fellow cohort members who were companions on the journey. And to all my friends, family, colleagues, professors, therapists, clergy coaches, and spiritual directors who had to hear me talk about this project *ad nauseum* for the better part of two years, thank you, thank you, thank you.

Glossary

1. **Attention Deficit Hyperactivity Disorder (ADHD):** A series of traits that, when present for a sustained period, will qualify a person for a diagnosis. The "official" symptoms of ADHD include Hyperactivity, Inattention, and Impulsivity though individuals with this diagnosis report experiencing several more common traits.

2. **Divergent Thinking:** Coming up with new ideas all the time, "connecting the dots" in ways most others cannot, finding a "third way" forward when groups are stuck.

3. **DSM:** The Diagnostic and Statistical Manual is used by professionals in the fields of psychology and psychiatry to diagnose mental health conditions.

4. **Emotional Dysregulation:** Has challenges tempering emotions, disproportionate feelings to situations, emotional outbursts, trouble naming emotions despite feeling them intensely.

5. **Hyperactivity:** Fidgets with hands, pens, or squirms in seat, especially during long meetings, leaves seat when expected to remain seated, feeling unendingly restless, unable to engage in activities for sustained periods of time (even activities one enjoys) is often on-the-go which many clinicians describe as a feeling of "being driven by a motor."

6. **Hyperfocus:** Ability to immerse oneself fully in work or a topic of interest for extremely long periods of time, sometimes forgetting to eat or use the restroom when fully engaged in something of interest.

7. **Impulsivity:** Talking excessively, interrupts or tries to complete others' sentences, difficulty waiting their turn, may intrude or take over what someone else is doing, thoughtless financial spending.

8. **Inattention:** Making careless mistakes, difficulty sustaining attention, seems to not be listening when others are talking (i.e. daydreaming), struggling to follow through on tasks, difficulty organizing tasks, losing things often, easily distracted by external stimuli, forgetful.

9. **Rejection Sensitivity:** When a person overreacts to the slightest real or perceived rejection or disappointment.

10. **Timeblindness:** Only two understandings of time—"NOW" and "NOT NOW," lacking an innate sense of time, grossly over- or underestimating how much time something will take, chronic tardiness.

11. **VAST:** Variable Attention Stimulus Trait. See ADHD

12. **Young Clergywoman:** A cis woman, trans woman, or femme identifying person aged 45 or younger who has worked for and received credentialing from a mainline protestant denomination.

Abbreviations

ADA—Americans with Disabilities Act

ADHD—Attention Deficit Hyperactivity Disorder

BOM—Board of Ordained Ministry

CHADD—Children and Adults with Attention-Deficit/Hyperactivity Disorder

ConEd—Continuing Education

CPE—Clinical Pastoral Education

DSM—Diagnostic and Statistical Manual

EAP—Employee Assistance Program

ELCA—Evangelical Lutheran Church in America

HIPPA—Health Insurance Portability and Accountability Act

IRB—Institutional Review Board

MHNP—Mental Health Nurse Practitioner

PCP—Primary Care Physician

PC(USA)—Presbyterian Church USA

PTO—Paid Time Off

SPRC—Staff Pastor Parish Relations Committee

UMC—United Methodist Church

UMCOR—United Methodist Committee on Relief

VAST—Variable Attention Stimulus Trait

Introduction

Shortly before I entered seminary, I heard public theologian Rev. Nadia Bolz Weber say, "You need to preach from your scars, not from your wounds." Weber is an Evangelical Lutheran Church in America (ELCA) pastor who rose to prominence after founding the House for All Sinners and Saints in Denver, Colorado and publishing several award-winning books. When I began forming my own theological identity as a budding seminarian and "baby pastor," she quickly became a meaningful voice for me. I took her meaning to be that if you are still "bleeding out" when preaching, metaphorically speaking, it will not only be messy, but also incredibly distracting to your audience. Perhaps you have experienced this.

I remember when the associate pastor at my home church was hired. She was fresh off a painful divorce and *every single sermon* she preached used her divorce as a "sermon illustration." Unfortunately, it came across as though she was using our congregation more as her own personal group therapy session. Thus, her open, gaping, wound left by her divorce overshadowed any hope of the congregation hearing her actual message.

This wisdom has stuck with me ever since, and in my own ministry I have tried to abide by it. Though preaching and writing are different,

Introduction

they are related enough that I adopted the same mindset as I approached my academic work and writing. However, as I was beginning this endeavor, I was diagnosed at age 34 with ADHD-Inattentive Subtype and my entire world turned upside down. Decades of exhaustion from masking natural traits, buried emotions from hiding the defining characteristics of my personality, and frustrations linked to the challenges I'd faced in work, academics, and my personal life were finally beginning to boil over. In other words, I felt like a grief-stricken, sadness laden, confused blob of a human for months on end after receiving my diagnosis. While in some ways receiving my diagnosis felt like a relief, in so many others it was wounding in ways I still cannot quite describe. The wound was fresh, and I barely knew how to talk about it with my family and closest friends let alone with professors, mentors, and colleagues.

However, as I discerned what I was being called to study and write, one thing, and one thing only kept rising to the fore: the abundance of clergywomen in my networks sharing that they had also been diagnosed with ADHD and their shared experiences of burnout. As both a clergywoman who has often thought about leaving ministry, and as a woman who received a "late-diagnosis" of ADHD in my mid-30s, I developed an insatiable desire to dig deeper into this topic, despite it feeling altogether too close to the surface for comfort.

My undying gratitude goes to my faculty advisor, Rev. Dr. Angela Yarber, who became a trusted sounding board and invaluable wayfinding guide on this journey. When I initially proposed this project, I voiced my concern that it may be "too close to home," and that I was unsure if it was wise to try and write about it (yet). Should I concentrate on something else first? At the time I was still deep in the throes of coming to terms with this new-to-my-consciousness diagnosis even though I had, apparently, been living with un-diagnosed ADHD my entire life. My medical team was still trying to help me figure out if medications might be beneficial, and I was still working with my therapist to find a new understanding of this condition. My struggle was real; I needed to start extending self-grace and compassion to myself.

Dr. Yarber, in her infinite wisdom, said something to the tune of, "I hear you... AND.... Sometimes we have no choice but to write from our wounds because we're living in systems that continuously wound us. We simply don't have time to heal. And writing can help us get there." So, with her blessing and encouragement, I set out to learn more about myself and my ADHD. Despite the fact that I felt like a gaping, emotional flesh wound, I set out to explore in depth how trying to navigate ministry with ADHD might be contributing to my persistent thoughts of leaving ministry.

Now, fully aware that I am still feeling wounded, while still striving for a better understanding of myself, (and praying for many of my wounds to heal), I offer this work to the church and to the world. I offer it in hope and prayer that it will be a gift to neurodiverse clergy-women, their churches, and church leadership as we continue to, as we United Methodists say, "strive for perfection." Because as well founded as clergy health initiatives, workshops, and retreats focused on "self-care" are, at the end of the day, neither I, nor any of my beautiful, amazing, talented, gifted, and *called* "neuro-sparkly" colleagues can self-care our way out of our diagnoses. Instead, we need to find a new way forward with our churches, colleagues, and leaders to increase the understanding of ADHD and to develop better ways to support neuro-diverse clergywomen—consequently improving the ways we can be in ministry with one another.

The burnout rate for ministerial professionals is higher than it has ever been. In early 2022, the Barna group found that forty-two percent of pastors seriously considered leaving full-time ministry.[1] And it was discovered years ago that clergywomen, at least in the United Methodist Church, leave ministry at a rate that is ten percent higher than their male colleagues.[2] These statistics are sobering at best, and highly discouraging at worst for those women who are beginning to discern a call to set apart, ordained ministry.

Over the course of the COVID-19 pandemic and the years follow-ing, yet another (possibly related) phenomenon has presented itself that I find wildly intriguing. During the pandemic, life slowed for

1. "Pastors Share Top Reasons They've Considered Quitting Ministry in the Past Year."
2. Ibid.

many young clergywomen. Slowly but surely a notable number of us began to discover that we had been leading our congregations with undiagnosed Attention Deficit Hyperactivity Disorder (ADHD). Did you know that ADHD is diagnosed at half the rate for girls as for boys in childhood? Yet in adulthood, men and women are diagnosed at approximately the same rate.[3] Some clergywomen had even been leading their congregations with other co-morbid mental health conditions in addition to their ADHD. This led us to reckoning with the fact that we had been making our way through our lives, our academic journeys, our relationships, and our careers without access to accommodations from which we could have benefited and to which we are legally entitled, at least in our professional lives and careers.

This experience, revelation, and struggle is one I know all too well: I was one of the many clergywomen who was diagnosed "late" during the pandemic, in my mid-30s, after having left at least two ministerial posts. Various clergy support networks through social media provided weekly if not daily evidence of this growing trend in 2020 and 2021. Clergywomen from all across the country were sharing stories of the challenges they faced in both ministry and their personal lives. Many were commiserating with each other and offering solidarity, support and resources. More than a few were telling tales about leaving their ministerial posts or being asked to leave abruptly and in ways that caused them tremendous emotional and spiritual harm.[4] Some of these social media posts and comment-thread conversations led others to speak with their care providers to begin the exploration of possible diagnosis because they related so thoroughly to these stories.

This was true for me as well. To a certain extent it was comforting to realize I was far from alone on this journey. Yet, even as I have now moved into a ministry context in which I feel I can thrive (campus ministry), I often find myself contemplating leaving the ministry altogether. I continue to face often overwhelming challenges due to lack of understanding of my diagnosis, and the subsequent lack of support I

---

3. "Women and Girls."
4. Horan, "Feminized Servanthood, Gendered Scapegoating, and the Disappearance of Gen-X/Millennial Protestant Clergy Women."

am offered. Outside support is critical to my success as I endeavor to navigate ministry as an individual diagnosed with ADHD.

In light of the growing awareness of the prevalence of ADHD in women in concert with the reality of the growing exodus of younger clergywomen from the ministry, this work explores:

1. The intersection between highly talented and capable young clergywomen diagnosed with ADHD who are leaving or contemplating leaving the ministry. "Young clergywoman" is defined here as those age 45 and younger as girls and women were not included in ADHD research for so long, resulting in many of us not being diagnosed until well into adulthood.
2. The support or lack thereof from denominational and church leadership for neurodiverse clergywomen and therefore all clergy.
3. Systems and structures that should be put in place to improve support for both neurodiverse clergy and their congregations or ministerial posts.

My hope is that by having explored these connections through qualitative interviews I have identified and clearly communicated strategies to improve support for neurodiverse clergywomen and education for adjudicatory leaders. In turn, denominations might therefore, over time, improve clergy retention, health, and vocational satisfaction. My interest in this research is heightened by the fact that I too am an ordained young clergywoman who has experienced living and leading with undiagnosed ADHD and has experienced the consequences of limited understanding and support by leaders, colleagues, and congregations. By investing in this work, the ripple effect to improve the pastoral-congregational relationship would be revolutionary, empowering both pastors and congregations to truly live into their collective call to work toward the transformation of the world.

Introduction

The themes explored are twofold:

1. Clergywomens' experiences, especially as they relate to disability and neurodivergence within the church.
2. The lack of support and training for adjudicatory leaders in supporting neurodiverse clergywomen and ways to improve understanding of this neurodiversity for the good of all.

My research questions were derived from my belief that the origin of much of the turnover and burnout for young clergywomen goes far beyond what most clergy health initiatives address. As we will discover in the pages to come, many women feel a call into ministry precisely *because* of their neurodiversity rather than *despite* it. Therefore, both churches and adjudicatory leaders simply need more education, training, and resources focused on how to effectively work with and support neurodiverse clergywomen.

While these women are talented and gifted in many ways, it is, as previously stated, less a need for self-care or clergy health initiatives, of which there are many, than a need for better understanding and support from leaders and congregations. To help illustrate this point and further explore these nagging questions I had beyond my own personal experience, I reached out through various social media channels and personal and professional networks to find study participants.

After several weeks of posting requests for interested clergy to contact me, I received inquiries from 16 interested clergywomen who met the parameters for participation. Of the 16 who expressed interest, 10 returned consent forms and scheduled a time to meet with me during the duration of the study. Using a qualitative interview methodology[5], I conducted ten qualitative interviews[6] via Zoom with other clergywomen who are aged 45 and younger, have been officially diagnosed with ADHD by a medical care provider, are ordained in a mainline protestant denomination, and have considered leaving ministry due to lack of support. I used the transcription feature on

---

5. Lindlof and Taylor, 172-173
6. Jacob and Furgerson.

Zoom to collect transcripts, which were later edited for clarity and then coded, both manually and with the help of the Delve program. Using a combination of inductive and deductive coding, a series of themes emerged, which provided the data set for this work.

Through this work, I want to encourage and empower neurodiverse clergywomen to name the root cause of their discontent with openness, honesty, and vulnerability; and subsequently be met with compassion, understanding, and support from their churches and adjudicatory leaders. With truth and vulnerability leading the way, my hope is that this work will pave a path forward to create new training and education, encouraging crucial conversations to take place between clergywomen, their churches, and their denominational leaders.

We will start in Chapter 1 by setting the stage and exploring what events brought me to the conclusion that I must focus my work on the intersection of clergywomen and neurodiversity. Chapter 1 also includes an outline of the eight ADHD traits that will be explored, complete with their definitions. Chapter 2 is an exploration of women in ministry and the challenges they face as compared to their male counterparts. In Chapter 3, we turn our attention to ADHD and how it manifests differently in women and girls as opposed to in boys and men. Throughout Chapter 4, I share my own story of receiving my diagnosis and begin to reflect on how it has affected my life and ministry. Chapter 5 contains a reimagining of the siblings from Bethany, Mary, Martha, and their brother Lazarus as a trio of siblings who each live with ADHD and its effects. Chapter 6 sets the stage for understanding the vocational realities faced by clergywomen with ADHD. Then Chapter 7 dives into the findings of the qualitative interviews and highlights the very real ways ADHD affects clergywomen and their ministries for both good and ill. And finally, in Chapter 8, recommendations are made for churches, church leadership teams, and adjudicatory and denominational leaders to increase support for the incredible neurodiverse clergywomen with ADHD they are entrusted by God to have in their midst and leading their churches.

Introduction

I hope that this work, this labor of love, will provide better guidance for leaders to support talented and called neurodiverse clergywomen whom, I would argue, the church *needs* for survival and growth. This in turn will help to create a culture within churches that makes it safe for neurodiverse congregants to also come forward and receive the care and support *they* need. That is one area in which research might continue to build upon this work—care and support for neurodiverse congregation members as well.

1. A Call to Curiosity

Uncovering the intersection of clergywomen and ADHD

The rate of clergy considering leaving ministry is larger than it has ever been. This is far from a new trend in the church. While exacerbated by the COVID-19 pandemic, there have been stories shared and research conducted by various educational institutions and church-adjacent research organizations such as the Barna Group and Pew Research about clergy burnout for years, if not decades. It's a never-ending pursuit to try and get to the root of the changing face of ministry and clergy burnout. Ministry is a vocation once regarded with a certain amount of respect and revered in some areas of the U.S., even in secular spaces. However, we now see clear trends in clergy leading almost all other professions in declining health outcomes and burnout rates.[1]

In the United Methodist Church, there is a growing disparity between the experiences and treatment of clergywomen as opposed to their male counterparts. Elizabeth Collier found as early as 1999 that "…the Division of Ordained Ministry of The United Methodist Church confirmed that women are leaving local church ministry at a ten

---

1. Proeschold-Bell and LeGrand, "High Rates of Obesity and Chronic Disease among United Methodist Clergy."

percent higher rate than male clergy."[2] While this finding could be a standalone issue, the fact that the way ADHD presents in women and girls differs from how it presents in boys and men, cross referenced with the different way that girls are socialized, is a key curiosity in this research. Does the combination of being a woman *and* having an ADHD diagnosis increase the stress of ministry and lead to higher rates of burnout?

While I am Ordained as an Elder in Full Connection in the United Methodist Church (UMC) and have a vested interest in improving the outcomes and experiences of clergywomen in the UMC specifically, this is far from an isolated issue. There have been studies on other mainline protestant denominations and the experiences of the clergywomen serving within them. In every single one, "these investigations have shown inequitable experiences between clergywomen and clergymen."[3] This fact is worthy of more study and research, as a major component of this reality is the embedded sexism and patriarchy of the institutional church. Unfortunately, this is borne of millennia of silencing women, going even so far as leaving many of their names out of our holy scriptures. Studying the sexism and patriarchal issues affecting clergywomen is best left for another day. This study will dive deeper into a subset of struggling clergywomen – those with the specific neurodiversity of ADHD.

ADHD, to be explored in more depth in Chapter 3, is a condition that affects every aspect of a person's life. By and large, ADHD is less a deficit of attention, but rather an over-abundance of attention paired with often ineffective or impaired executive functioning which affects the control and regulation of our attention. While there could be a multitude of reasons that "a study… revealed that clergywomen experienced discontent in their interpersonal relationships with their superiors, peers, and parishioners,"[4] I posit that an underlying cause for a not-small percentage of clergywomen is very likely undiagnosed or diagnosed but undisclosed and misunderstood ADHD.

---

2. Collier, "United Methodist Clergywomen Retention Study."
3. Ibid.
4. Ibid.

Furthermore, it has been found that "clergywomen experienced overt discrimination, lack of acceptance, and were stereotyped into certain gender roles"[5] within their churches and careers. And it is precisely the presence and pervasiveness of societal gender roles and the way society (at least in the U.S.) socializes little girls and women that has kept the discovery of ADHD in many of us hidden for so long. Another intriguing facet of ADHD is its differing presentation in women which we will explore later in this work.

Of all the things that jumped out at me as I read the Collier Study on United Methodist clergywomen retention rates, one that resonated most deeply was the conclusion of the research that "…women do not seem to be getting the support they need from the hierarchy or their congregations. Flexibility on the part of churches and the appointment (UMC) and call systems (most other mainline denominations) is in order and could be beneficial to both the clergywoman and the congregation."[6] My own experiences of leading my local congregation or extension ministry area, while simultaneously working with my District Superintendents and cabinet and striving to navigate the appointive process in a way that I can be both faithful to my call and the institution as well as to myself and honor my own needs (medical, physical, mental, emotional, and spiritual) has proven to be true.

The more I learn about myself, the way my own unique brain is wired, and the many varied ways ADHD affects every aspect of my life, the more I ponder ways denominational leaders, colleagues, and churches might be better equipped to understand and support neurodiverse clergywomen. Just as many other jobs and institutions make accommodations possible for employees with disabilities as outlined and mandated by the Americans with Disabilities Act (ADA), so too must the church begin to adapt and strategize for the greater flourishing of all within its care. Neurodiverse clergywomen called to lead the church into the future for the transformation of the world are deserving of similar accommodations.

The reality of a growing clergy shortage will not be news for

5. Ibid.
6. Ibid.

anyone in mainline Protestant Christianity. The "Great Resignation" following the Covid-19 Pandemic did not skip the realms of church or ministry by any stretch of the imagination. Many denominations have poured resources into studying this trend and creating clergy health initiatives and doubling-down on their adamancy that clergy focus on their self-care. I continue to assert that the church is missing the mark, especially in the case of their neurodiverse clergy. While they push self-care and throw everything they can at the symptoms they observe but might not fully understand, next to nothing is done to treat the core issues. In the case of neurodiverse clergy, misunderstanding and a lack of support for those who naturally engage with the world differently is apparent.

I am living proof that, even with a strong self-care regimen in place, many clergy continue to struggle due to entirely different factors than not taking all their PTO or neglecting to make regular doctor's appointments. Case in point, the feedback on my commissioning interview with the conference Board of Ordained Ministry lauded my self-care, which included taking my sabbath day consistently, using both my PTO and continuing education time in full every year. Additionally, I was diligent in keeping regular therapy and spiritual direction appointments. I had cultivated a robust support system outside of my parish including family and friends and activities unrelated to work such as a weekly improv class and volunteering as a Girl Scout leader in my local community (which allows me to camp regularly, another necessary component of my own personal spiritual-care regimen).

Despite all my follow-through on the many and varied clergy self-care recommendations made by both my conference, seminary, and touted by mentors as crucial to a successful ministry, I still burned out in my first appointment in a monumental way. Of course, there was no shortage of systemic-level issues at play such as problematic family-system dynamics within the congregation and financial challenges that were far outside the bounds of my control. Yet there were other elements and recommendations that, despite some excellent advice from mentors, I simply couldn't carry out regardless of my best efforts.

For example, I found myself impulsively sharing information with too many people in spite of my best efforts and intention to keep sensitive matters to myself. I struggled not to take bad behaviors by church members personally. Ultimately, I left feeling rejected by this congregation that I loved and wanted to be with and felt called to lead. It was not only heartbreaking but nearly broke my spirit and sense of self as well. My sense of call came under serious internal scrutiny for months following my departure.

It has taken me several years of reflection, therapy, and internal processing to realize that most of my own perceived shortcomings in that ill-fated appointment were simply exacerbated by my undiagnosed ADHD. Receiving an official diagnosis by a medical professional was integral to my healing as I worked through the aftermath of those two years. For example, my oversharing with so many different people was a classic sign of *impulsivity*. My inability to "let things roll off my back," was made far worse by the *rejection sensitivity dysphoria (RSD)* that many women with ADHD report experiencing. RSD left me feeling as though *everything* was a statement on my worth as a human being.

Without the knowledge that I was trying to manage ministry and ADHD, and lacking the crucial support, coping strategies, accommodations, and medication I now have access to, I did not have the ability at the time to understand or regulate myself fully. Nor was I able to advocate for myself in a way that might have increased my leadership team's understanding of my needs, potentially easing the pain and reducing the harm of that situation for both myself and the congregation. Although I eventually would have left that congregation, the insights and self-awareness gained since that time through my late ADHD diagnosis have helped provide a much-needed new perspective. It has allowed me to cultivate a whole new level of self-compassion when I look back on that season of my life and ministry.

> Rejection Sensitivity Dysphoria left me feeling as though everything was a statement on my worth as a human being.

It was during the global crisis of the COVID-19 pandemic and subsequent slow-down three years into my credentialed ministerial career that my own usual tips, tricks, and strategies for success finally began to crumble in a way that I could no longer ignore. For many women with late-diagnosed ADHD, this shift often happens at earlier points in their lives, such as when they go off to college and are no longer being kept on a schedule or watched as closely by parents and teachers and instead are faced with having to organize themselves in a new way for the first time. For others, it is when they become parents or are given more responsibility at work and have their usual coping mechanisms stretched beyond what they can maintain. Yet I had moved away for college, lived abroad, and finished a master's degree all prior to the point of realization that something was inexplicably "off."

After I left my first church appointment, I shifted into hospital chaplaincy. I completed my first unit of Clinical Pastoral Education (CPE) and immediately after began a year-long CPE Residency. Between the new and pressing stressors of a global pandemic and the compounding pressure to complete my ordination paperwork and prepare for my Board of Ordained Ministry interview, it became almost impossible to function as I once had. Not to mention the fact that I was still adjusting to an abrupt and unexpected job change into a realm of which I knew little (hospitals and healthcare). All my usual coping strategies fell short, and I was no longer able to "mask" my ADHD, even from myself, in the same ways I had apparently been doing, unwittingly, for decades.

In consultation with my therapist at the time, I first began an anti-anxiety medication that helped to "take the edge off" for a few weeks. This was prescribed once she noted that the situational anxiety I was experiencing, precipitated by the extensive preparation needed for my ordination paperwork and impending "big, scary interview," warranted attention and treatment. I am distressed to this day that it was the anxiety of my United Methodist ordination process that led to my realization that I needed medicinal support for anxiety rather than the very real emergency of the global pandemic. It is indicative, I believe, of a broken system that is partly to account for the over-whelming burnout of clergy. Young clergy, especially, are so stressed by the ordination process they're already so fatigued at the outset of their careers it's no wonder so many leave expeditiously.[7]

However, after those first few weeks on the anti-anxiety medication it soon felt as though my brain was "broken" in a new and alarming way. It felt as though I was looking at all the tools I knew I needed to get through this stressful season of life, and all that I had in my metaphorical toolbox, but my hands were now somehow too slippery to grasp, let alone use any of them.

Then, two key things shared via social media in the early months of 2021 nudged me into thinking that I might be one the many women who had been "missed" in childhood for an ADHD diagnosis. One story was from another clergywoman who, in reflecting on her own "late" ADHD diagnosis and a previous pastoral post that had gone awry, shared that she believed that she had been in an "ADHD spiral." She ended up leaving her congregation abruptly to go on a medical leave of absence. In reading her story, many of the experiences she shared were akin to what I recalled experiencing in my first appoint- ment. She shared challenges such as impulsively sharing too much about what she was facing with too many people, having trouble regu- lating her own emotions, and feeling rejected by her congregation to the point where it felt physically painful. I remember feeling as though I could have written a very similar post in that forum and as though the phrase, "ADHD spiral" was jumping out at me as the descriptor I had been looking for to help me articulate that season of my life and ministry to others for years.

The second was a friend whom I had met through the creative outlet of improv classes a few years before. She shared an article enti- tled *"The Lost Girls,"* from The Guardian in which the author, Noelle Faulkner, reports about her own experience of being diagnosed later in life with ADHD-Inattentive Subtype.[8] She highlights in the article the difference of ADHD presentation between boys/men and girls/women, and it was the first place I was introduced to the obser-

---

7. Collier, "United Methodist Clergywomen Retention Study."
8. Faulkner, "The Lost Girls: 'Chaotic and Curious, Women with ADHD All Have Missed Red Flags That Haunt Us.'"

vation and assertion that part of the reason girls are missed for ADHD diagnosis in childhood is because of the way we, especially in western cultures, socialize little girls.

For those of us with ADHD-Inattentive Subtype, we are often seen as good girls who are simply "daydreamers," or "overly sensitive,"[9] rather than girls who are desperately in need of help and access to resources that will help us focus, regulate our emotions, and stop talking to ourselves so negatively, fervently believing that we will never amount to anything. Upon reading this article, I knew beyond the shadow of a doubt that it was time to talk to my therapist, a trained professional, about whether I might be one of these "Lost Girls."

For weeks I worked with my therapist to explore my childhood and earliest memories. I recounted challenges at school and at home, academic and relational. We began to explore the internal narratives and "scripts" which had been running on a continuous loop in my mind for most of my life. Almost all the narratives were negative and self-deprecating, telling myself I was lazy or not trying hard enough. Often berating myself for not knowing how to better control my big emotions. Wondering why I couldn't just be "normal" like everyone else. Lamenting that I felt on the edge of every friend group I had rather than like a member of any core group of gal-pals.

Most of my internal monologues, we found, were practically a textbook example of how girls and women with undiagnosed ADHD tend to internalize the messages we often receive about being "too sensitive," "lazy," or how we're "not meeting our potential." With my therapist's blessing, I began to seek out a psychiatrist with the ability to perform a fuller diagnostic assessment. By the spring of 2021, I had an official diagnosis of Attention Deficit Hyperactivity Disorder or ADHD-Inattentive Subtype.

Although ADHD was a condition which I had heard about and had passing familiarity with due to my years as a youth leader and camp counselor, it usually brought about thoughts and images of elementary-aged boys, and the "Inattentive Subtype" was a presentation of ADHD that I had never heard about despite apparently living with it

---

9. Ibid.

my entire life. Only through the course of this research did I learn that the reason for this very likely has to do with the fact that ADHD research including girls and women lagged behind the research centered on school-aged boys by several years if not decades.[10]

Suddenly, I felt both validated and bewildered. Within a matter of days, it seemed as though my whole life had been turned upside down. While I was still me, it felt as though I was a whole new person that I had to meet and rediscover and try to understand in a totally new way. For the first time I had an explanation for so many of my quirks and habits, thought processes and challenges, both academic and professional, as well as throughout my personal life. As I began to reflect on my life in conjunction with throwing myself into research about ADHD, so much of my life began to make sense in a way that it never had before.

Not long after I received my diagnosis, I was surprised by a deep grief that settled in for my younger self. I wondered how it was that so many adults in my life had missed the fact that I so clearly had ADHD and could have benefited from support, therapy, perhaps medication, and certain accommodations at school. Although I understand cognitively that a large part of it is due to the lack of research on girls and women in this field, I still struggle emotionally. It is a grief that I continue to work through even now as I discover ways both large and small that ADHD has affected my life, academic career, self-efficacy, spiritual wellbeing, relationships, and vocational pursuits.

It wasn't long into my self-research and quest for more information before I began noticing a related trend in my personal and collegial networks. I appeared to be one among many women under the age of 45 who were receiving a "late" diagnosis of ADHD. Stories began to pour forth in several areas of my life from friends and colleagues sharing similar stories from their jobs or home lives. None intrigued me more than my fellow clergywomen. Story after story of "failed" pastorates, moving from one job to another, and no shortage of relationship woes were shared in online forums and in quiet conversations in coffeeshops and during phone dates and Zoom calls.

---

10. Crawford, "ADHD: A Women's Issue."

Uncovering the intersection of clergywomen and ADHD

All of this felt eerily familiar, as though I could have written or told these stories myself. At the very least I felt a deep sense of solidarity with these colleagues and their struggles. Could the unnervingly large percentage of young clergywomen burning out of the ministry be explained in part by missed or late ADHD discoveries and the lack of support from churches, colleagues, and denominational leaders? I began to wonder.

Then I read the recounting of a conversation Thom Hartmann had in the mid-1990s with an Indian physician and two Indian businessmen while traveling through central India as shared in his forward of Kate Kelly and Peggy Ramundo's book *The ADDed Dimension*. In the conversation he asked the gentlemen if they had ever heard of "Attention Deficit Disorder." (The diagnosis name has changed and evolved in the Diagnostic and Statistical Manuel since the 1990s.) While at first confused, after he explained the condition, the Indian physician nodded sagely and shared that in his country, they call people such as Hartmann described, "old souls." He remarked how strange he found it that while his country classified people with ADHD as spiritually mature, those in the United States classify those persons as having a "disorder."[11] For the first time I felt truly seen. Through a conversation between physicians on a train in India, that transpired 20 years ago, it suddenly warmed in my own heart, mind, and spirit, *of course* women with ADHD would be called into ministry!

We are, by all accounts, "old souls" as the Indian physician described. We simply engage the world differently than others and see everything through a lens which allows us to see connections that others do not. We are hyper-empathetic and can pay attention to a multitude of people and activities simultaneously. The things others struggle with are the very things at which we excel. Skills such as staying calm in an emergency or thinking so far outside the box ("what box?") that no one else has seen the connections or thought of the solutions we suggest.

All of this and more uniquely qualifies us for the hard and holy

---

11. Kelly and Ramundo, *The ADDed Dimension: Celebrating the Opportunities, Rewards and Challenges of the ADD Experience.*

work of ministry. For the first time, I reconsidered whether my fellow ADHD colleagues and I are the ones that need to change or improve the way we do ministry. Instead, I began to imagine a future where churches and denominations realize the absolute gift they are receiving when a neurodiverse clergywoman is appointed or called to their congregation or ministry setting—and the golden opportunity they have to blaze a new trail by working to better understand and *support* their neurodiverse clergy. I began to envision a more accepting and bearable world for those who are simply wired a little differently than the rest. For we *are* created in God's own beautiful and unique image. Why couldn't this work start in the church, especially as we begin to reframe neurodiversity as a *spiritual gift?*

To this end, the invitation to participate in this study was issued to clergywomen with ADHD from a variety of mainline protestant denominations. The invitations were issued primarily through Facebook via a post I placed in several private groups that were comprised of young clergywomen, women with ADHD, and clergywomen with ADHD. Participants were invited to opt-in by emailing me and completing a short questionnaire to ensure they met the requirements of identifying as a woman, being ordained in a mainline protestant denomination, were age 45 or younger, and had an ADHD diagnosis that was determined by a medical professional. Those women who were selected for the study met all requirements, assured me they had appropriate self-care measures in place (therapist, spiritual director, etc.), and returned a consent form per IRB requirements prior to scheduling their interview.

Since I am but only one person with a single lived experience to share regarding living and serving in ministry with ADHD, this research has been strengthened by the completion of ten qualitative interviews with other young clergywomen who have been living and serving with ADHD and who have either left or contemplated leaving active ministry due to the challenges they faced.

Research participants are all young clergywomen as defined as those age 45 and younger. The reason for this somewhat older definition of "young" is because so many of these women, like me, were not diagnosed until their mid-30s or later when many of our denominations no longer classify us as "young." They had to have a verified diagnosis of ADHD and were able to reflect upon how their ADHD has affected their ministries. They were also asked to imagine and articulate the ways in which they envision a future where congregations and denominational leaders are educated on the needs of those living with ADHD and better equipped to understand and support neurodiverse clergy. All of this was pursued with the goal of improving support for clergy and the relationships between clergy, their churches, and their denominational leaders.

In addition to asking each participant, generally, how ADHD has affected their ministries, we explored eight of the most commonly experienced and *noticeable* traits of ADHD. The use of the word *trait* here is highly intentional as the field of ADHD research expands and discovers more about how our brains are wired. For too long, those with ADHD have been told that it is our "behavior" that is a problem and absorbed messages that the things we struggle with are choices (bad ones) that we are making. These messages are incorrect, ill-informed, and cruel as it is not our behavior that those around us notice but rather our natural *traits*. This is simply the way God made us, in God's own image.

> ...it is not our behavior that those around us notice but rather our natural traits. This is simply the way God made us, in God's own image.

In the first half of the interviews, we explored how each of these traits beneficially affect the clergywomen's ministries as well as how they pose challenges. Then, in the latter half of the interviews, we explored how we imagine churches and church leadership both at the local and adjudicatory levels might become better informed and thus equipped to increase their understanding and support for neurodiverse clergy.

The eight most noticeable ADHD traits we investigated included[12]:

---

12. Hallowell, *ADHD Explained.*

DSM traits of ADHD:

a. **Inattention:** making careless mistakes, difficulty sustaining attention, seems to not be listening when others are talking (i.e. daydreaming), struggling to follow through on tasks, difficulty organizing tasks, losing things often, easily distracted by external stimuli, forgetful

b. **Hyperactivity:** fidgets with hands, pens, or squirms in seat, especially during long meetings, leaves seat when it is expected to remain seated, feeling unendingly restless, unable to engage in activities for sustained periods of time (even activities one enjoys) is often on-the-go which many clinicians describe as a feeling of "being driven by a motor"

c. **Impulsivity:** talking excessively, interrupts or tries to complete others' sentences, difficulty waiting their turn, may intrude or take over what someone else is doing, thoughtless financial spending

Commonly experienced and reported traits of ADHD in women:

a. **Rejection Sensitivity:** when a person overreacts to the slightest perceived rejection or disappointment

b. **Emotional Dysregulation:** challenges tempering emotions, disproportionate feelings to situations, emotional outbursts, trouble naming emotions despite feeling them intensely

c. **Hyperfocus:** ability to immerse oneself fully in work or a topic of interest for extremely long periods of time, sometimes forgetting to eat or use the restroom when fully engaged in something of interest

d. **Timeblindness:** only two understandings of time – "NOW" and "NOT NOW," lacking an innate sense of time, grossly over- or underestimating how much time something will take, chronic tardiness

e. **Divergent Thinking:** coming up with new ideas all the time, "connecting the dots" in ways most others cannot, finding a "third way" forward when groups are stuck

Uncovering the intersection of clergywomen and ADHD

As this project becomes a usable resource across denominations, it will be important to ground the work in sound theological exegesis. It should expand through employing creative theological imagination. Therefore, I have chosen the biblical family of Mary, Martha, and Lazarus of Bethany. I reimagine them as a family of siblings that very well may have all had some form of ADHD. We now know the condition is highly genetic – if one family member is diagnosed it is likely that others will be as well, or may be living, as I was, with the condition but undiagnosed and under supported.

The first seeds of the creative theological reimagining of Mary of Bethany as a biblical figure who might have been living with a neurodiversity were planted within me by a colleague and mentor years ago. More than a decade before my own "late" ADHD diagnosis, I was hired on to do some consulting work with our local United Methodist campus ministry to help their residents find a more amenable way of cohabitating in community. When I entered the executive director's office to discuss how we would approach the strife within the student community, I was taken aback by a beautiful, large needlepoint portrait hanging above her desk. The image was of a young girl who clearly had Down syndrome and was smiling serenely at the viewer. I asked about it and learned the campus ministry's director, an artist, had crafted the piece herself and, most interestingly, it was her interpretation of Mary of Bethany.

Prior to her post as executive director of the campus ministry, Rev. Dr. Melanie Reuter had done her own doctoral work studying the narratives of Mary and Martha. In her creative theological imagination of their story, she questioned why Martha had a home of her own. It is an interesting piece of the story, given that women were highly unlikely to have homes of their own. Culturally, a woman was considered property and therefore would have lived in either her father's or her husband's home. And although the birth order of Mary, Martha, and Lazarus it is never clearly stated, the text indicates Lazarus is the only male child and would be the one to have received their father's inheritance. It is curious, then, to note that the text clearly says that Jesus went to *Martha's* home, not to the home of Lazarus.

Due to these factors and the way in which Mary is presented in the two major pericopes in which we hear about these siblings, this colleague re-imagined that Mary might have had a condition such as Down syndrome. In the scene in which we first meet this family, Jesus comes to visit. While Martha is busying herself with the many tasks of hospitality, Mary sits at his feet and listens to him. Often this leads to preachers and teachers interpreting this story as Mary doing the "right" thing and Martha being "distracted" doing many things which is alluded to as "wrong." However, in this reimagining, Reuter suggests that Martha has been tasked by their parents to be Mary's caretaker. She gained Lazarus' permission to split the inheritance, to afford Martha the ability to be self-sufficient yet able to care for both herself and Mary in exchange for giving up whatever life she might have imagined for herself. In this way, the story changes from one of Martha being distracted to one of Martha being mindful that Mary fared better when keeping to a scheduled routine, as we now know benefits many individuals with Down syndrome.

Likewise, thanks to modern medicine, we also know a great deal more about Down syndrome and how those with the condition have some of the biggest, most loving hearts of anyone you will ever meet. Reuter points this out and suggests that in the story where Jesus is called to Martha's house once again, this time upon the occasion of Lazarus' death, it is the display of emotion pouring forth from Mary that moves him to raise Lazarus from the dead. This theory is corroborated by her following observation that Mary is the woman who pours the costly perfume on Jesus' feet at the dinner following the raising of Lazarus and that a person with Down syndrome would not be concerned with the cost or perceived "wastefulness" of this gesture; rather, such a one would be wholly focused on the love and care being poured forth on the object of their affection.[13]

When I first heard these reinterpretations of the stories of the sisters from Bethany, I recall feeling goosebumps. Truly, I felt in my heart, mind, and spirit that there was something to this creative theological interpretation and it has clearly stuck with me for the better part of 16

13. Reuter, Melanie. 2008. *The Three Marys: A Workshop on John Wesley's Way of Salvation.* Washington, D.C. Wesley Theological Seminary. 2008.

years. In this work, I would like to build upon this reimagining and reinterpret once again the siblings Martha, Mary, and Lazarus. Rather than imagining only one sibling with a disability, what if all three of them had a condition that was not well understood at the time and affected every aspect of their day-to-day lives?

It is known now that ADHD is a highly genetic condition, and if one sibling is diagnosed there is a higher chance that their siblings will be as well. And we know from the narrative in the Gospel of Luke during Jesus' presumed first visit to their home, Martha is up and down and all around the house, portrayed as a kind of busybody who can't sit still. What if Martha had an ADHD-Hyperactive Subtype presentation whereas Mary, more prone to sit serenely and daydream while trying to listen to Jesus had ADHD-Inattentive Subtype? And, to take it a step further, we might imagine that Lazarus too had ADHD-Combined Subtype.

While modern biblical scholarship has done much for women, people of color, immigrants, the LGBTQ community, and other marginalized populations to see themselves reflected in scripture, less has been done for those with physical disabilities and even less with so called "invisible disabilities" such as ADHD and other types of neurodiversity.

Representation matters, and it is important for all people to see themselves reflected both in the world today and in the portrayal of characters in the Bible or their own holy texts. While modern biblical scholarship has done much for women, people of color, immigrants, the LGBTQ community, and other marginalized populations to see themselves reflected in scripture, less has been done for those with physical disabilities and even less with so called "invisible disabilities" such as ADHD and other types of neurodiversity. In her book *The Disabled God*, Nancy Eiesland forges the first inroads to exploring the presence of people with disabilities in the Bible. She imagines how that might affect the word and work of the church in the world today as an advocate for ALL of God's beloved children to be able to live their lives in wholeness. She leads the way in helping persons with disabilities be seen as also created fully in the *Imago Dei*, the Image of God.[14]

In the pages that follow, in addition to my own story, I will share

---

14. Eiesland, *The Disabled God: Toward a Liberatory Theology of Disability*.

the stories of 10 clergywomen that have worked to navigate life and ministry with ADHD, most of whom were diagnosed later in life. Their stories will both break your heart and provide you with tremendous hope. Through them, you will see a new face of God and a whole population of clergy who have been misunderstood and undervalued for most of their careers. We will explore the miscommunications and misunderstandings that continue to arise because ADHD research took so long to include girls and women. Finally, we will imagine a new way forward for doing life and ministry together.

These women have helped to provide creative and illuminating suggestions for churches, church leaders, and denominational leaders to consider as they strive to provide the best possible care and support for their clergy. Only by listening to each other and working to learn about the lived experiences of others can we hope to bring about transformation in the world and in the church. While the project starts here, I hope that this may be the first of many steps in exploring how those with diagnosed conditions defined as "neurodiversity," or as I like to call us, "neuro-sparkly," might be more fully welcomed and affirmed within the church for the glory of God and the transformation of the world.

2. Gender and Ministry
Navigating the weight of an uneven pulpit

Before we jump directly into exploring the effects of neurodiversity on the ministerial careers of young clergywomen, I believe we must first explore the ways in which simply being a woman in ministry is a challenge in and of itself. As I was beginning seminary, I recall being informed that the average length of time first-career clergywomen were staying in ministry was about five years.[1] Due to the immense undertaking pursuing a master's degree is, both intellectually as well as financially, this was a startling and somewhat disheartening statistic to hear. I was feeling so sure of my call into vocational ministry that I saw no other option than to begin that journey, especially as I had received a full tuition scholarship from my seminary of choice.

For me, seminary was a time of incredible affirmation of my call and my skills for ministry. I was surrounded by both peers and professors who saw and called out gifts in me that I rarely took time to notice or appreciate within myself. We do tend to be our own worst critics, and ADHD, I have come to find, can exacerbate that tenfold. It was a shock then, when in my first appointment, which I will share more about in Chapter 3, I was told by my Staff Parish Relations Committee

---

1. "How Many Quit? Estimating the Clergy Attrition Rate."

(SPRC) that I should never be ordained. One person even had the audacity to say to me that it was "such a shame," that I would still have a job after I left their church. All of a sudden, I felt the statistic of the five-year mark being the point in which clergywomen tend to leave ministry in an entirely new and visceral way. I am, unfortunately, in good company, as the Barna Group's research on clergy retention rates show that "the immense stress of the job," and "feeling lonely and isolated" are top reasons clergy consider leaving ministry.[2] Let me tell you, nothing will make you feel more lonely or isolated than having people you trust, love, and respect look you dead in the eye and tell you they think you shouldn't be credentialed for the very vocation to which you feel wholly called!

My tenure with that church took place prior to the COVID-19 pandemic and, while there were certainly stressors both within and outside of our little local church from finances to floods, there were even larger stressors brewing. Between the COVID-19 pandemic and the turbulent political terrain in which clergy were having to navigate preaching and pastoral care, there was an uptick of thirteen percentage points of pastors who considered leaving full-time ministry between 2021 and 2022 settling in at 42%.[3]

This data is similar to that which I have gleaned from the 10 clergy-women who agreed to be interviewed for this project. (All participant names have been changed to protect confidentiality). One of the questions I asked each of them in the middle of each interview was, "Have you ever thought about leaving ministry? And if so, do you believe those thoughts are due to, or exacerbated by, trying to manage ministry with ADHD?" Out of the ten interviews conducted, five of the participants shared that they have indeed considered leaving full time ministry, and all five of those participants did cite the challenges of managing ADHD in professional ministry as a stressor. Interestingly, one of the women currently works in an academic setting rather than a local parish. She views this role as ministry and believes the schedule in that context is more conducive to living with ADHD, while another

---

2. "Pastors Share Top Reasons They've Considered Quitting Ministry in the Past Year."
3. Ibid.

shared, she has thought about leaving ministry but did not believe those thoughts to be precipitated or exacerbated by her diagnosis but rather by the unhealthy nature of the church which she was serving at the time she had those thoughts.

While not currently expressing thoughts of leaving ministry, Pastor Louise had this insight to share regarding the challenge of trying to manage her ADHD while also managing the abundance of expectations from her churches and church leaders. She said, "… maintaining this kind of pace as a neurodivergent human is inhumane. It's not healthy."[4] She continued to muse about the systemic challenges in churches today, especially ones that tend to be clergy-centric, with unreasonable and unrelenting expectations placed upon their pastor. Furthermore, she voices the desire for more time for rest for clergy, be it increased vacation allotments or more opportunities to take voluntary leaves of absence to recharge and recenter oneself, especially as a clergyperson who needs extra time to re-regulate an often-dysregulated system.

While the rate of clergy burnout and the statistics regarding those who consider leaving ministry are concerning across the denominational board, I am particularly concerned as a United Methodist clergyperson about the heightened rate at which we are seeing this within our own denomination. In addition to the Barna study on clergy retention, the Anna Howard Shaw Center at Boston University has also been exploring this trend. It is beyond disheartening to learn from their work that, in the United Methodist Church specifically, "…the Division of Ordained Ministry of The United Methodist Church confirmed that women are leaving local church ministry at a ten percent higher rate than male clergy."[5]

While the reasons for this are varied, I have no doubt that an underlying cause of this larger number is the overlooked prevalence, misunderstanding of, and thus lack of support for clergywomen with ADHD. For it is our ADHD that makes us some of the most creative, innovative, and empathetic clergy any church could hope to have

---

4. Louise, "008.Louise."
5. Collier, "United Methodist Clergywomen Retention Study."

leading them. This is something we will explore in-depth in later chapters, but for now let us look at the differences between how men and women are perceived in their pastorates as leaders.

While men who move quickly on ideas and take the lead on new initiatives are seen as "good leaders," and "innovative," similar women by contrast are labeled "bossy," "pushy," or seen as too "impulsive," which for clergywomen with ADHD may be a critique that cuts especially deep as impulsivity is simply a natural trait that we possess by virtue of living with this condition. Likewise, clergymen who can't sit still or who interrupt others or are otherwise always on the go are "gregarious," and "charming," while clergywomen are "tiresome," or labeled "busybodies." While ADHD presents differently in men and in women, the societal expectations and descriptions used vary widely between the sexes, and all too often the descriptors and thus perceptions of women lean heavily negative. Is it any wonder, then, that the research shows time and time again that women who have been living with ADHD often present with anxiety and/or depression first, as these messages become internalized and eat at us from the inside out? Sometimes this goes on for decades before anyone realizes that, hey, we were just born this way.

Without travelling too far down the rabbit trail of unequal pay or the disparity between the experiences clergymen and clergywomen often have with parishioners and church leaders alike, it does need to be stated that inequitable experiences between clergywomen and clergymen abound. [6] This was highlighted in a powerful way by the North Carolina Synod of the Evangelical Lutheran Church in America (ELCA) in 2018 when they put out a short video entitled "Seriously?"[7] in which several male clergy were asked to read, on camera, statements that their clergywomen colleagues had submitted of things that had been said to them either by parishioners or male clergy colleagues. Statements from how the clergywomen were dressed to statements that would count as outright sexual harassment were read. As the clergymen participating were asked to read the statements without having

---

6. Ibid.
7. *"Seriously?" Women in Ministry Video.*

seen them first, it was quite telling how disturbing some of the comments were as a few of the men had trouble reading them aloud.

> The fact that any neurodiverse clergywoman is still in the ministry at all is nothing short of a miracle.

It should come as no surprise, then, that many of the clergywomen I interviewed shared their thoughts about leaving vocational ministry while also holding in tension how difficult they would find leaving to be. Pastor Ruby pointed out how challenging it would feel to walk away from ministry after having received a terminal degree in the field. Yet she recounted how "getting my position, I had to scrap my way into it, because I'm a woman in ministry, and that's usually the way."[8] Imagine that, on top of being a woman in a male-dominated field in ministry, you are also a woman with ADHD. Your brain never stops whirring, you have trouble focusing, and you are always working at least as hard as anyone else in the room to finish at half the pace they do. If clergywomen are leaving ministry at a ten percent higher rate as clergymen in the United Methodist Church, how much higher might this rate be for our neurodiverse clergywomen? The fact that any of us are still in the ministry at all is a miracle.

Many of us have also chosen to stay not because of, but despite our experiences in ministry. Here we are not only talking about the experiences we have in our local churches where we are appointed or called, but also our experiences with our regional and denominational leaders. While I can only speak for myself, it does seem that, as long as one of these two entities is supportive, clergywomen are more likely to find ways to cope and stay in the ministry. However, if *both* their local church *and* their adjudicatory leaders are unsupportive, then this creates a precarious and often unsustainable situation, even for the most self-aware, healthy, and well-regulated clergy.

The way that this played out in my own ministry, and what led me to seek a job outside of the local church, was when I got so sick during my first appointment that I ended up hospitalized for pulmonary

---

8. Ruby, "001.Ruby."

emboli (blood clots in my lungs). While my medical team never quite figured out the genesis of the blood clots, my primary care physician to this day remains convinced that the stress I was under trying to manage my first congregation without much support from my regional leaders was a pertinent complication that we need to continue to keep our eye on. In fact, he still jokes with me at every annual well-visit and asks if I'm ready for him to write a doctor's note for my "permanent file," that would disallow me from ever reentering a local church pastorate. While I appreciate his concern, this saddens me a great deal that a care provider who has known me as long as he has (he was my pediatrician so he's known me since childhood) can so clearly see the toll that my vocation is taking.

I still remember the feelings I had while sitting in a meeting with my regional leadership shortly after being discharged from the hospital. My recovery was slow-going and I was not yet up to full speed and simply exhausted. And this was years before I realized that I was also dealing with an undiagnosed condition that can be, by all accounts, exhausting in and of itself. The crushing feeling of thinking I was a failure as, with a distinct tone of disdain, my regional supervisor asked me, *"Well, what, do you think you need a medical leave?"* In that moment, I felt about four inches tall and not at all empowered to speak up for myself or my needs.

In hindsight, the rejection sensitivity dysphoria was working over-time and the mere thought of disappointing my regional leadership was anathema to my brain, heart, and spirit. Pastor Elizabeth and I discussed the feelings we get when we try to advocate for ourselves and how nice it would be to be met with support rather than looked at like we have "four heads because of a developmental disorder."[9] The intersectionality of being a woman and being diagnosed as neurodiverse in any way only adds to the strain of the uphill climb succeeding in ministry (whatever that means) often feels like.

While I am neither married nor have children, clergywomen who do have even more, or at least different hurdles to overcome in ministry. Yes, being single has its own set of challenges and comes with

---

9. Elizabeth, "002.Elizabeth."

its own plethora of... commentary... from well-meaning church folk who are prone to asking inappropriate and prying questions. One of the questions I do not have to field, though, are questions regarding how I plan to balance being both a pastor and a mom. I know plenty of clergywomen who have been asked this either on their road to ordination in their interviews or from search committees, or, most infuriatingly, even from their own denominational leadership. While the questions may be asked with the intention of being caring and concerned for our wellbeing, these questions are at their root sexist and discriminatory. Unless ordination committees and church leaders are asking the same of our male counterparts.

While the information that being a clergywoman comes with certain challenges may be nothing new to those of us who have been hanging out in the church for some time, I hope that it adds a helpful backdrop to where we will be heading from here. In the same way as many churches and parishioners are still working on overcoming their own

> Our abilities to think outside the box, hyperfocus, and be so deeply in touch with our emotions, making us profoundly empathetic, are nothing short of superpowers for ministry.

internal biases regarding women being ordained as clergy (even though we've been doing that since 1956, at least as Methodists) the stigma surrounding mental health and neurodivergent diagnoses add an additional layer of trepidation for those of us endeavoring to be faithful to our call to ministry while navigating inherently human systems.

One of the primary goals of this book is to help break the stigma surrounding ADHD, and to help churches and church leadership begin to see the incredible giftedness in their neurodiverse clergywomen. Our abilities to think outside the box, hyperfocus, and be so deeply in touch with our emotions, making us profoundly empathetic, are nothing short of superpowers for ministry. On the flip side, these traits come with a cost and that often is in the form of extreme energy output, even if it's all internal and others may not see or notice what a monumental lift keeping ourselves regulated and healthy is. In a similar vein as the Clergy Retention Study, I posit that [neurodiverse] clergy "...women do not seem to be getting the support they need from the hierarchy or their congregations. Flexibility on the part of churches and the appointment system is in order and could be beneficial to both the clergywoman and the congregation."[10] Let's explore the ways that we might increase support for the benefit of all.

---

10. Ibid.

3. Hidden in Plain Sight

The gendered presentation of ADHD in women and girls

Now that we have explored the ways in which gender affects the experiences of clergywomen in comparison to our male counterparts let's take a look at the differences between men and women when it comes to ADHD. If anyone had asked me prior to 2021 to define ADHD, I, like many others, would likely have described a child, probably a boy, who has trouble staying in his seat in school, can't focus, and by all accounts appears to have more energy than his poor little body can contain. And, in part, this is a correct description. ADHD often does present in a primarily "Hyperactive" presentation. This is only one of the ways it can appear, and in 2021 I was shocked by my diagnosis to learn not only did I have ADHD, but that I had the primarily Inattentive Subtype, something I didn't even know existed!

As I previously shared, when I was first exploring my newly identified anxiety with my therapist, a friend of mine posted an article from The Guardian on Facebook entitled *"The Lost Girls"*[1] which proved to be a pivotal read in my diagnosis journey. In the post she shared that she had just discovered that she had been living with undiagnosed

---

1. Faulkner, "The Lost Girls: 'Chaotic and Curious, Women with ADHD All Have Missed Red Flags That Haunt Us.'"

The gendered presentation of ADHD in women and girls

ADHD and had recently received a "late" ADHD diagnosis in her 30s. As I read the article, more out of curiosity than anything, I was shocked at how much of the article seemed to be describing... well... me. One of the quotes pulled from the article and placed in big BOLD letters in a pop-out on the website read, "The assumption is that ADHD makes little boys disruptive. But it can also make little girls feel like they'll *never be good enough.*" (emphasis mine).

Wow. For the first time I saw the tiniest glimmer of hope that perhaps, finally, I might be headed toward discovering the reason why I have spent the entirety of my life feeling like a complete and total outsider. From my earliest memories, I've always had a sense that I just don't "get" life in the same way as those around me do. Whether it was feeling more comfortable talking to my teachers than to my peers, refusing to join the "in crowd" when I knew they were making others feel left out, being the last to turn in my daily work and every test or quiz I've ever taken in my life, or never feeling like a part of a cohesive group of friends, there has always been a sense I've had that I don't "fit in" in any way. In high school a friend of mine and I even called ourselves the "Elementary Rejects" given how we had felt throughout our earlier years.

> "The assumption is that ADHD makes little boys disruptive. But it can also make little girls feel like they'll never be good enough."
> - *Noelle Faulkner*

The article gave a wide overview of many of the differences in presentation of ADHD between boys, girls, men, and women and the further I read, the more and more sense it all made. It also said that girls were not included in ADHD research until the late 90s and were not included in any kind of longitudinal study until as late as 2002—at which point I was already a freshman in high school! No wonder so many of us women who are receiving what is coined as "late" diagnoses are called the "Lost Girls." We endured years of academia without anyone thinking that we might have been having many of the same struggles as the boys in our classrooms, but that it was simply manifesting differently within us.

Every facet of one's life, the article said, is affected by ADHD. And although "attention deficit," is one of the key phrases in the official name of this condition, any expert will be quick to tell you that it is an incorrect description. Rather than a deficit of attention, those of us living with ADHD actually experience an overabundance of attention. The challenge or disability comes in the inability to effectively or consistently *regulate* that attention. This leads to challenges in our academic and professional pursuits, our relationships, and in our ability to manage our daily lives and homes. This is to say nothing of being able to keep up with the world around us due to the sheer amount of energy we are constantly using to try and manage the chaos within.

The flip side of the challenges of ADHD is an abundance of creativity, emotion and empathy, curiosity and stamina. Bringing awareness and understanding to the benefits of ADHD is a necessary component of any plan to help individuals and churches and other organizations better understand and support their ADHD leaders. It is also why I so appreciate the work being done by author and expert Edward Hallowell who suggests a change in the name of this condition. Rather than ADHD which, in this "deficit-disorder model of ADHD; pathology written into its very name, reinforces the image of ADHD as an affliction with few, if any, saving graces,"[2] he suggests the term "VAST"[3] as those of us living with it in reality, "tend to have great talent embedded in great struggle."[4]

From the first chapter in his most recent book, *ADHD Explained,* Dr. Hallowell introduces and explains his hope of changing the terminology this way in a section titled "What's in a Name?":

People ask me all the time, 'What's the difference between ADHD and ADD?' Back in 1981, when I first learned about this condition, it was called Attention Deficit Disorder, ADD. Just a few years later in 1987 the name was changed to Attention Deficit Hyperactivity Disorder, ADHD. And the condition was officially divided into subtypes. You could have ADHD with or without hyperactivity. But this division confused everybody

---

2. Otsuka, *ADHD For Smart Ass Women.*
3. Hallowell, *ADHD Explained.*
4. Ibid.

because instead of one type, ADD, and the other type, ADHD, it was decided to discard the term ADD altogether. Technically, in diagnostic terms, ADD does not exist. Instead, if you have ADHD without hyperactivity the diagnosis you are supposed to receive is ADHD Primarily Inattentive. And if you have ADHD with hyperactivity your diagnosis is ADHD Combined Type. More than 35 years this nomenclature still confuses people. I think we need a new name for this condition because not only is the term ADHD inaccurate it also implies cognitive impairment, as if the condition was similar to dementia, or to the ears of the layperson, as if those with ADHD are just not very bright. Therefore, I would like to propose a new name that incorporates three of the key elements of the condition: variability, attention and the search for stimulation into one term—Variable Attention Stimulation Trait, V. A. S. T. or VAST. After all, the condition is indeed vast. The term is accurate; one we could be proud to use. And it doesn't make us feel substandard as if doors are closed to us, which is absolutely not true.[5]

In support of this movement, for the remainder of this work I will employ the term VAST rather than ADHD except when quoting others. I agree with Dr. Hallowell that VAST is a term that I would feel proud to use, and that shifts my own self-understanding and internal narrative from one of self-deprecation to one of self-love and acceptance. In theological terms, I also prefer the term VAST as I think about those with this trait being created in the image of God, an image that is diverse, vast, and entirely beyond human comprehension.

One of the most intriguing arguments the article from The Guardian made was that, in many ways, it was not simply the oversight in excluding girls and women from the official research that has led to a delay in diagnosis of this condition in half of the population, but also the very way that girls and women are socialized that has kept us hidden and flying under the radar for so long. For decades, if not centuries, girls and women have been socialized to "be a lady," and

---

5. Ibid.

told that we should be "seen but not heard." These expectations of girls and women then pair well with the fact that so many of us have the Inattentive version of VAST where the 'hyperactivity' we experience is primarily within our own brains, and the rejection sensitivity that is so often a hallmark of our condition keeps us in line and terrified that if we step out of line then we will upset someone whose approval we are desperate to either obtain or to keep.

One of the core memories I hold from my time in elementary school is that while many of my friends were pegged as what our school district called "Gifted and Talented," I was not one of those students. That meant that, for several years in elementary school, a group of my friends were in the "GTE" or "GTA" (Gifted and Talented Education and Gifted and Talented Art) programs. These groups met early one or two days a week at one of the other elementary schools, and then they would come into class all together laughing about whatever had happened that day and creating their own memories, inside jokes and deeper friendship bonds and such. Oh, the longing and FOMO (fear of missing out) that I felt in those days. Not being a part of the GTE crowd made me feel like I was not measuring up to my full potential, and that I was somehow not as good as everyone else around me. While no adult ever explicitly said this to me, the reality that there was a "special" program that was titled "Gifted and Talented," and I was NOT in it was clear enough, even if unintentionally so, for my young brain at the time to get the message—I wasn't *gifted*. I wasn't *talented*. *I wasn't good enough.*

This was around the same time that I was in second grade where our daily routine was to come into class and the first thing we were expected to do was to finish a certain amount of self-paced "morning work" before lunch time. While enough time has passed that I can no longer remember the specifics, I vaguely recall there being a daily grammar lesson and number of math problems that needed to be completed. If these items were not done by lunchtime we were told that we needed to stay in and finish them after lunch before we would be allowed to go out and join our classmates at recess. Unfortunately, the place where we were told to sit and complete this work was not back in a quiet classroom, but instead at one of the lunch tables in the loud and noisy cafeteria. And not just at any lunch table, but at a lunch table that had a bright laminated sign above it that read,

"MAKE A BETTER CHOICE."

That's right, those of us who worked a little slower than our peers, and who were more distractable, were lumped in with the behavioral discipline "troublemakers" and expected to sit with them in a noisy cafeteria to finish our work. It was not exactly a recipe for success, let me tell you. I cannot recall exactly how much recess I missed in second grade, but it still feels like it was far more than was necessary. And in retrospect I am appalled that I had to sit at that insensitively named table on more days than not. My deep gratitude goes out to Sherri Conrad, my gym teacher at Lakeside Elementary, who took the time one day that year to sit down at the lunch table with me and say to me, "Katie, I'm really sorry that this table is named the 'Make a Better Choice Table,' because it's not your choice to be here. You simply work slower than others, and that's OK." Ms. Conrad, you have no idea how reassuring those words from a trusted adult were to me then and how they have stuck with me for decades, acting as a counterbalance to all the messages society tries to throw at me that I'm "stupid," "lazy," or "not living up to my potential."

Another core memory of elementary school was my fifth-grade year where I was decidedly NOT in the "in crowd" in my homeroom. There was a clear girl's group in fifth grade and everyone in the entire grade knew who was IN and who was OUT. Now, I was one of the lucky ones as I was not often a target of the bullying that was common coming from that group. It appeared everyone agreed that I was a nice enough classmate, but I was not at all "cool" enough to be "in." However, if you had tried to tell my little sensitive self back then that I was NOT being bullied, I wouldn't have believed you. For what I now understand to have likely been my rejection sensitivity dysphoria was working overtime that year. I was crushed day in and day out to know that, for reasons unknown to me, I wasn't included with the majority of the girls in my class. This was most viscerally obvious in the winter months when we had a lot of indoor recess.

I can still see clearly in my mind's eye most of the girls from both fifth-grade homeroom classes convening in the back of my homeroom classroom, talking and laughing together. Meanwhile, there were three other far smaller groups of girls. There was me and my friend, who happened to use a wheelchair, who hung out together on the far-left side of the classroom (as you face the teacher's desk) near the classroom sink, pencil sharpener, doorway and cubbies. Another two girls almost directly across from us on the far-right side of the classroom, one of whom often wandered over to me to ask me to be her emissary to ask the girls in the back if they would let her hang out with them (a request I denied time and time again). And lastly, three girls front and center, who were their own safe little trio of musketeers.

In hindsight, it was probably the three girls in the front whose group I most wanted to be a part of because they were nice, and I knew the girls in the back were 'mean girls.' Whatever it was about that age and stage of my development and the effects of VAST that were not yet known to be a contributing factor, my fifth-grade year left lasting emotional scars that I hate to admit I am still having to work through to this day.

Throughout my interviews with the other clergywomen who had to navigate early elementary, middle, and high school years with VAST (whether known or not), I learned that I am far from alone. True to much of the research, it appears as though most of us were internalizing the messages that were either said directly to us by the adults in our lives who didn't understand us, or by society at large that we internalized and later turned into shame that we are now working to overcome.

Pastor Gloria recalls seeing an interview with Tom Cruise, self-identified Scientologist, but incredibly well-known public figure, where he said in an interview that he believed that ADHD, and psychology as a field as a whole, was a crock. The fact that such a public figure was going on national television spouting that sort of stigma paired with her parents' direct comments calling her "lazy," left a lasting impression.[6] Likewise, Pastor Fiona recalls that she viewed

---

6. Gloria, "006.Gloria."

herself for most of her childhood as "flighty," thinking less of herself and making "dumb blond jokes," at her own expense to try and hide the shame she was feeling.[7]

Prior to deciding to concentrate on VAST as a research topic as I pursued my Doctor of Ministry, and thus prior to any of the interviews I later completed, the "Lost Girls" article ignited a curiosity in me that I had not felt for a long time. A season of research began as I sought to find any and every resource I could get my hands on that would help me better understand the ways that VAST presents in women as I tried to figure out if this might be something for which I should be tested. Much of my information came from the organization Children and Adults with Attention Deficit/Hyperactivity Disorder, or CHADD. This organization provides education, advocacy, and support for individuals with VAST and their families. By signing up for their digital newsletter, I began receiving at least weekly articles in my inbox that expanded my knowledge and awareness about VAST, and I also was able to register for several free webinars to learn from experts.

CHADD has an entire section of their website dedicated to information about the symptoms of VAST in Women and Girls.[8] It reiterated and confirmed that what I had read in The Guardian article was indeed true. Women and girls have been overlooked and underdiagnosed when it comes to VAST precisely because of the differences in the ways it presents within us, paired with the overwhelming societal expectations and stereotypes that swirl around us. Who would ever think that a girl who seems either excessively chatty or conversely like she has her "head in the clouds," always daydreaming, might be experiencing hyperactivity and racing thoughts that she can't seem to control? And in a culture, at least here in the United States, which is my own context and frame of reference, where women are already often seen as less-than in the workplace, why would a lack of close attention to detail or inability to sustain attention in long meetings ever raise any 'red flags' for anyone?

The further and further I got down the VAST rabbit hole, the more

---

7. Fiona, "003.Fiona."
8. "Women and Girls."

and more fascinated I became, and the more committed I became to learning as much as I could about how this condition was likely affecting me and so many of my colleagues. It wasn't long before I began wondering how the dots might connect and began wondering if all the well-intentioned clergy health initiatives and self-care seminars might not be working to treat the symptoms of a much deeper root issue. What if the high rates of clergy burnout, especially among women, were less to do with our gender, as has often been the reason given, but instead due to a lack of understanding and thus support for our uniquely wired brains?

As this wondering settled within me the curiosity grew and grew until I had no other choice but to propose this as my research topic. Between the pandemic and the increase in diagnoses I saw shared among my colleagues it became a timely passion project. Once I was given the green light, I set out to start finding research participants. Since so many women are not diagnosed until their 30s, I set the age limit, in consultation with my faculty advisor, at 45. Some might say this no longer qualifies as "young clergy," but given the reality that many of us are less than 5 years out from receiving our diagnosis it felt appropriate.

I also did not want to limit my research to only the United Methodist Church, so I named "Mainline Protestant" as the parameter, widening my potential participant pool. Finally, I needed to be sure that each participant had a qualified medical professional that had given them an official diagnosis. While it can be easier (and cheaper) to 'self-diagnose,' for the purposes of this project, an official diagnosis was required. And with that I set out to get IRB approval, created a 10 question interview and began recruiting participants. The themes and patterns that were awaiting me were clearer than I could have ever imagined them to be.

4. Personal Narrative as Lived Inquiry
Diagnosis, identity, and pastoral formation

The path to my own late diagnosis of ADHD—Inattentive Subtype was not unlike many women's journeys. First diagnosed with circumstantial anxiety, further digging and exploration with my therapist at the time led us to wonder if there might be a deeper underlying root cause. At the time I was meeting with a therapist through the Employee Assistance Program (EAP) provided by the hospital where I was completing a Clinical Pastoral Education (CPE) residency. CPE, for those who are unfamiliar, is an intensive program where chaplain trainees are expected to complete clinical hours meeting with patients and their families providing spiritual care as well as many hours of coursework with class at least once a week. During those weekly classes, trainees discuss assigned readings, present verbatim accounts from their patient encounters, write and present papers and presentations, and participate in "IPR," or "Interpersonal Relations" modules where the cohort is expected to bring up and deal with any conflict within the group in real time.

Many find CPE to be a tedious process, and many students balk at the idea of having to confront, explore, and understand their emotions at that deep level. For me, however, CPE made me feel as though I was in the right place. Perhaps due to what I now understand as my own emotional dysregulation, I LOVE talking about my emotions and trying to figure out what they are and why I'm feeling them and how to best manage them in real time. In the middle of the second unit of my residency the world was hit with SARS-COV2 which precipitates COVID-19. To put it mildly, working as a student chaplain who was very new to hospital work during a global pandemic was…stressful. And as the world grappled with what was going on and many civilians refused to follow best practice advice, the amount of rage I felt was unparalleled, and in instances quite disconcerting. I'd felt angry before, but never at this level and never quite that consistently or for that long a period.

As chaplain trainees we were navigating incredible uncertainty. This period was also prior to the availability of vaccines so the anxiety about whether we might get sick and what would happen if we did was very real. We were journeying alongside patients, family members, staff and even supervisors as we faced the unthinkable. It would make sense, then, to assume that I was in therapy at the time and being diagnosed with "circumstantial anxiety" to help manage the incredible stress of my day-to-day work life.

My friends, it is with great lament that I tell you that, no, it was not the stress or anxiety of learning how to be a chaplain during a global pandemic that precipitated my need to be prescribed anti-anxiety medication for the first time in my life. No, it was my *ordination process* that did that. You see, the United Methodist ordination process is notoriously cumbersome, lengthy, rigorous, and has a bad habit in many areas of burning candidates out before they complete the process and are ordained. I was already coming to the end of my second mandatory year of provisional membership between commissioning and ordination and, in addition to a full time chaplain residency, had also picked up a part time middle school youth leader position at a local church. I had done this because, according to our denominational polity, to be qualified to apply for ordination, clergy must serve two probationary years under full time appointment; the status of full or part time is dictated by the amount of our paychecks, not the hours we are working.

So, to recap, while I was discussing my increasing anxiety as I prepared for my ordination interview with my therapist, I was working 60+ hours a week in two separate locations, one of which was a hospital during an unprecedented (in our lifetimes) global pandemic and preparing for what, in my mind, was my *BIG SCARY ORDINA-TION INTERVIEW*. Due to the heightened anxiety everywhere, when I went in to see my primary care physician and his nurse practitioner, they were quite amenable to providing a prescription. In many ways, starting the anti-anxiety was helpful, "the edge" was taken off, and I was living in less of a constant panicked state. But, very shortly after I began the anti-anxiety medications, other things began to feel "off," in ways that they never had before.

It turned out that, for me, the anxiety—likely a byproduct of the undiagnosed VAST—was helping in many ways to mask the VAST. For years, it turned out, it was the anxiety that was a counterbalance to the VAST "timeblindness" that has kept me showing up early for decades to everything from doctor appointments to low-key house parties. But without the anxiety I was running late to every meeting and appointment on my calendar. The anxiety of fearing how people would perceive me in group or public settings was now gone, and suddenly I was more impulsively interrupting people and blurting out almost any thought that came into my head. I was simultaneously feeling more like myself than I ever had and the most *unlike* myself as I ever had.

Within about six weeks of my therapist suggesting I might be experiencing some circumstantial anxiety was when the two women from two entirely different sectors of my life posted on Facebook sharing their own recently diagnosed VAST. One posted The Guardian article that spoke of the prevalence of undiagnosed VAST in girls and women and the other was a trusted clergywoman who shared in a private group her reflections on a previous pastorate. In hindsight, she could see how her VAST had affected her ministry and her ability to cope with a challenging church now that she had received an official diagnosis. This post grabbed my attention as it sounded eerily similar to my recollections of my own first appointment. The phrase that jumped out to me most viscerally was when she shared that she believed she may have fallen into what she named as an "ADHD Spiral." Something about this term felt akin to what I had experienced as well. It was as if I could have written her entire post myself.

In my first appointment as a "greenhorn" pastor, things went with alarming speed from manageable to bad to worse in my second year with that community. Early in my second year the local community served by this church was hit with what was described as a "50-year flood." The sanctuary of that church was on the second floor specifically because there had been a history of flooding in that area. We immediately teamed up with the local food bank, the fire department, the police department, other area churches and businesses, the civic association, and several community activists and began serving free weekly meals. Lowe's also donated needed supplies, and we became the location where the local arm of the United Methodist Committee on Relief (UMCOR) dropped off "Flood Buckets" for our community members to come and pick up.

I remember flying into super-pastor mode in those weeks. My brain was lit up with excitement and intrigue and seemed to thrive in that crisis. Where others were freezing and wondering, "What do we do? How do we help?" I was actively making phone calls and connections and making strides to get the word out in every way that I could that our church was a safe place for people to come and use the restroom, get a hot meal, take a break, and pick up whatever supplies we could provide for their continued efforts to salvage their homes. The local news even came and interviewed me that week!

Within two months of that and feeling as though I was really thriving as a new pastor, everything shifted. Apparently, some members of the congregation didn't appreciate that I'd opened the church to our neighbors. Others were disgruntled that I refused to ask the parents of our youngest children to take them out of the sanctuary on Sunday mornings and instead insisted that ALL are welcome at church. The tight and stressful finances of that congregation notwithstanding, there were several things "going sideways" simultaneously. And, in hindsight, I can see how my deficiencies in executive functioning, a hallmark of VAST, were not helping. I couldn't seem to prioritize needs. My hyperfocus on welcoming children and families likely did make me appear to be less than receptive to other generational needs within the church itself.

The most debilitating things in that season, however, were my inability to "grow a thicker skin," and the fact that I couldn't seem to stop telling anyone within a 10-foot radius of myself everything that was going wrong at that time and asking for their advice. In one phone call with a specifically chosen mentor who had high level skills in employee supervision, I recall he told me that I needed to be very careful who I spoke to about the insubordination I was receiving from multiple staff members. As I kicked the pebbles in the parking lot in which I was standing during that phone call I remember thinking to myself, "I'm not sure I can stop myself." And, as I feared, over the next several weeks whenever anyone would listen it was like the filter in my brain was malfunctioning, if not missing entirely. Despite knowing logically that I shouldn't be sharing with them, I couldn't keep my mouth closed. It was infuriating to not know why I couldn't stop myself from oversharing—and I did not yet have the awareness to know that impulsivity, another trademark of VAST, was at play and unmanaged as I did not yet know that I was living with an undiagnosed condition.

As I reflected deeply on my own first appointment and the traumatic experience it became, in concert with the post I had read by a colleague and the article posted by a friend, I began to wonder if I might not have VAST too. At my next therapy appointment, I broached the subject with my therapist who spent the rest of our session performing a deep dive into my childhood. Memories from elementary school and feeling like I was always an "Elementary School Reject," came to the fore. I could remember how viscerally I felt the sting of feeling like the only one no one wanted to play with at recess. The sign that read, "Make a Better Choice" hanging over the lunch table in second grade, where I had to sit almost every day to finish my morning work before being allowed to go out to recess, was burned into my memory. I recounted for her how I seemed to always be the very last student to turn in any test or worksheet, was always on the fringes of every social group, and how I'd never felt as though I had a friend group to claim as my own. I recalled how devastated and inconsolable I had been at different points in my childhood and adolescence when I wasn't chosen for teams, or cast in the spring musical, or felt rejected by unrequited love interests. And let's not bring up how I felt about my ACT score!

By the end of that session, my therapist shared that, while she didn't have the credentials to test me, she would support me if I decided to seek out a diagnosis. When I went in for testing, it felt as though I didn't know what part of the test was and what might have been a cruel irony. The ticking of the clock in the psychologist's office was particularly distracting to the point I had to pause in one section of the tests to ask her if the clicking tock WAS the test, or if it was an oversight, as it was so distracting to me, I couldn't concentrate on the task at hand. By the time I returned for my read-out of my results, I was so thoroughly convinced that I had VAST I was truly unsure how I would react or what I would do if she told me I didn't have it.

It was in April of 2021 that I received my official diagnosis of ADHD-Inattentive Subtype (VAST) and began reviewing my life through this new and enlightening lens. Suddenly, I wasn't just someone who was "too sensitive," or who was "lazy," or who displayed "repeated patterns of behavior." Instead, I was someone who, for years, decades even, had been trying her best to keep up with all the other kids. Who had studied twice as hard to do half as well as her peers. I rediscovered an inner child who was cut so deeply by the smallest of (or perceived) slights that it routinely became impossible for her to concentrate on anything else. An inner child who, for her entire life, hadn't had the ability to communicate to others that while others might be able to let things "roll off their back," to her it felt like there was instead an internal tape player on loop in her head that would relentlessly play all her faults and failures back to her again and again. Along with a wave of relief, there was a wave of grief for my younger self when I received my diagnosis.

Throughout this time, I noticed an undeniable trend of other women within my age group sharing that they too were receiving "late" VAST diagnoses. Some were seeking testing in conjunction with realizing their children were presenting with symptoms. Others, like me, had been slowed down enough or thrown so far off their normal routines during the pandemic that the skills and masking tactics that they had always used were no longer enough to cover up that there was something more going on. And nowhere was this phenomenon more noticeable or concerning than it was with my peers, other clergywomen.

As a member of Young Clergywomen International, a professional organization that "creates a holy and authentic community that sustains generous collaboration, embodiment and solidarity for and by Christian clergy women under 40,"[1] I was privy to several quiet conversations happening online and in Zoom rooms and during small gatherings where clergywomen were disclosing this new discovery about themselves. It was in these spaces that we began providing solidarity for one another as we were on a journey of relearning how our own brains are wired, reflecting on our respective challenges in ministry, and trying to establish new and healthier ways to cope and care for ourselves. And it was what inspired me to begin wondering whether there may be an unrealized correlation between the high burnout rates and *neurodiverse* clergywomen.

---

1. www.youngclergywomen.org/about

5. Rereading Bethany
Reimagination and neurodivergent possibility

Have you ever noticed how so many of our Bible stories seem to only be interpreted and shared in one or two certain, predictable ways? Sometimes the continuity of hearing different pastors, churches, and every Bible Study group I've ever been in tell familiar Biblical stories the same way is a great comfort. In a world that is always changing, these consistent touchpoints can serve as a needed respite of familiarity and reprieve. Unfortunately, if we continue to share the same stories and interpret them in the same way we, as Christians and people of faith, will remain stuck. Which I'm afraid will then lead to limiting our own view and experience of God, and who God is trying to tell us they are. Which is why, when someone can introduce me to a new way of thinking about a familiar text or interpret a well-known and well-loved story in a new and surprising way instead of getting angry or trying to fight whatever discomfort that might introduce, I endeavor to approach the new idea(s) presented with curiosity and openness.

This is the experience I had over a decade ago when I asked a colleague about a beautiful portrait hanging above the desk in her office. While you couldn't see it from the hallway, if you entered her office and turned around you were greeted with a serene portrait of a young girl who, even in two-dimensional form, gave off the distinct aura of peace and tranquility. The portrait was quite large, and when I looked at it closer, I realized it had been cross stitched. This was, I knew immediately, a labor of deep love. I asked my colleague about it, and she invited me to sit while she shared about her own doctoral research and project which had focused on the "Three Marys"—Mary the mother of Jesus, Mary Magdelene, and Mary of Bethany. This portrait, she said, was her own interpretation and envisioning of Mary of Bethany.

This comment gave me pause because, while it was indeed a beautiful and serene portrait, it was evident that the little girl within it was someone with Down syndrome. Down syndrome, or Trisomy 21, is a genetic abnormality where a person is born with three copies of the 21st chromosome rather than the usual two. While individuals with Down syndrome do face several developmental and physical challenges, they are generally able to live long and happy lives. As I had grown up with a friend whose older sister lived with Down syndrome, I knew immediately upon seeing this portrait that its subject had Down syndrome. The news that it was a depiction of Mary of Bethany was what took me by surprise.

In the well-known stories of Mary and Martha, their brother Lazarus and their friend Jesus, we learn quite a bit about them. We "know" (or at least I've always been told) that these three are siblings, that Martha is a "busybody" who needs to learn how to take a break, and Mary is a daydreamer who would rather sit and listen to stories than help prepare the house for respected guests. We know Lazarus died and that Martha and Mary expected their friend Jesus to come to their aid more quickly and to do more before their brother's death. And by all accounts, they were angry and wasted no time in chastising Jesus when he finally showed up late (or so they thought), before Jesus appears to bring Lazarus back from death and out of the grave.

Rev. Dr. Melanie C. Reuter, Martha's Sister Mary, needlepoint on canvas, 20" x 20"

"Did you ever notice though," my colleague asked, "that it says that Jesus went to *Martha's house*? Not Lazarus' house. *Martha's* House." We discussed how in biblical times it was not common for women to have their own homes. Women were still considered property and were given from their father's house to their husband's house, often with a large dowry in what was more akin to a business exchange than the celebrations of love and holy covenanting that we know today when we think about marriage.

During this discussion, I realized I had never noticed that before. Nor had I ever realized that the biblical text does not provide a birth order for these three siblings. For whatever reason in my mind, I had always just thought that Lazarus was the oldest, Martha was the middle sibling, and Mary was the baby of the family. Of course I have

> Imagine that it was not one, but instead all three siblings (Mary, Martha AND Lazarus) that were living with a condition that affected every aspect of their lives and inhibited their ability to live fully independently.

no proof of this, it was just what I always assumed. Their birth order is beside the point, because in those days, no matter where in the sibling lineup he landed, as the only male sibling it would have been *Lazarus* who would have inherited their father's home and land and whatever savings or assets the family had. In any other story, Jesus would have been going to *Lazarus' House*. Or perhaps it would have been phrased *The House of Lazarus* as it often was.

In her doctoral thesis, Rev. Dr. Melanie Reuter outlined and shared an entirely new interpretation of Mary and Martha and their brother Lazarus. She imagined a world in which Mary may have been born later in their parents' life, and that with Lazarus' blessing as the rightful (in that time) heir, provided Martha a house of her own in exchange for her forfeiting her right to any life other than one in which she would become Mary's primary caretaker.[1] Truly this is perhaps one of the most creative and non-traditional interpretations I have ever heard in regards to this story, and it is clearly one that has stuck with me now for nearly two decades. I would, however, like to take the imaginative interpretation a step further and imagine that it was not one, but instead all three siblings that were living with a condition that affected every aspect of their lives and inhibited their ability to live fully independently. Yet, somehow, the strengths and shortcomings of each fit together just perfectly enough that, by living together with Martha as the head of the household, they live meaningful, happy and healthy lives despite the societal expectations and stigmas they routinely faced.

Let us imagine for a moment that Martha, rather than being a "busybody," as she has often been interpreted, is instead living with

---

1. Reuter, "The Three Marys."

ADHD-Hyperactive Subtype. Instead of being an overly controlling "Type-A" personality who would rather chastise her sister for not helping her with the housework and women's work of waiting on their honored guest, she is transformed into someone who, instead of being seen as rude, is now someone who is simply internally compelled to keep moving. If Martha were to be diagnosed with ADHD-Hyperactive type, she could simply be feeling as if she is being "run by a motor" at all times. Even when she might want to stop, sit, and simply listen to Jesus, there is a dysregulation of her focus and energy, and she simply can't turn it off or regulate her energy at will. This, while sometimes problematic, is what helps their household run because while she can't regulate her constant movement, it is what allows her to attend to the many tasks of keeping their home running. She is the sibling who can follow through on the cooking and the cleaning and the going to the market and paying their taxes and temple tithes on a regular basis.

Martha is also, in this telling, the sibling who observes the others the most closely. And in her years of being the primary caretaker for her sister, Mary, she has realized that Mary does best when she is kept on a regular schedule. If left to her own devices, Mary, who is living with undiagnosed ADHD-Inattentive Subtype, would spend most of her days unaware of the passage of time, forgetting to eat at regular intervals and overlooking most of the housekeeping needs. Without prompting and gentle guidance from her sister Martha, Mary would fall further and further behind her peers. Even as women were not often going to formal education in the same way as their brothers, fathers, uncles, and cousins were, Mary would have fallen behind in learning the domestic skills taught by the older women in their community and would have struggled to keep relationships of any kind—friendships or otherwise. It would be hard for their father to find a husband for her and given her higher needs and Martha's acumen about how to best care for her sister, the thing that made the most sense was to ask their brother, Lazarus, if he would be willing to share his inheritance to ensure his sisters' wellbeing.

Lazarus, who conceivably was living with ADHD-Combined Type himself was more than happy to agree to this arrangement. Not only did he love his sisters very much, but he also knew that without husbands of their own when their parents died, he would be the one left to take care of them. Unfortunately, Lazarus finds it hard enough to take care of himself. He often gets so absorbed at work to the point where he will look up and hours will have passed, and he realizes that he has forgotten to eat any meals all day. He rarely remembers to go to the market, and when he does, he either buys far too much or not nearly enough. His finances are often askew and the thought of having to one day support his sisters is so overwhelming it's nearly paralyzing for him to even think about.

By accepting his father's request and in collaboration with his sisters, they contrive a subversive system that benefits them all, completely working around the social norms of their day. They set up households in Bethany that are close enough to each other so that, even after they leave their father's house, they can continue to work together to take care of each other. Lazarus providing the needed oversight and permission for things the women need, and his sisters ensuring he stays well fed and his home livable, as he likely also is not a top contender for marriage given his absent mindedness and overfocus at work.

In her seminal work *The Disabled God*, Nancy L. Eiesland brought to the attention of Biblical scholars and theologians the limitations of reading scripture exclusively through a lens which, even if subconsciously, assumes abled bodies as the "norm." She writes:

> A reconception of the symbol of Jesus Christ, as disabled God, is developed here as a contextualized Christology. It is contextualized in that the disabled God emerges in the particular situation in which people with disabilities and others who care find themselves as they try to live out their faith and to fulfill their calling to live ordinary lives of worth and dignity. Contextualization is an authentic process of perceiving how God is present with people with disabilities and of unmasking the ways in which theological inquiry has frequently instituted able-bodied experience as the theological norm. The theological lenses through which we have traditionally viewed our own and

others' bodies distort the physical presence not only of people with disabilities but also of the incarnate God. To contextualize then is to both engage the past and present of a biblical text or a religious symbol in light of the past and present of its readers and hearers and to look to the future and the transformative effect that such a reading can have upon those who will come into contact with it.[2]

While Eiesland focuses her work primarily on physical disabilities and the need to read scripture through a disability lens, she does provide a nod to "hidden" disabilities as well. This is where I have endeavored to pick up the mantel as the same argument is, I believe, highly transferrable here. VAST and other neurodiverse conditions are classified as disabilities, and those of us who are diagnosed with them need to be given permission to see ourselves in our sacred texts. Seeing neurodiverse people in scripture is also important for those around us who may never know we have a disability unless we choose to disclose it. Our challenges may not be as immediately evident as seeing a wheelchair or seeing service animals trotting alongside those with physical handicaps, but they are no less real and no less valid.

While Eiesland reinterprets Jesus Christ as the disabled God, using the story of Mary, Martha, and Lazarus is just as powerful. Perhaps a closer look at the life of Christ and a reconception of a "Neurodiverse God" or "Neurodiverse Christ" is in the offing sometime in the future. For now, however, let us remember that, if we truly believe that "all persons are made in the image of God," then these three siblings are yet reflections of the divine Creator. Why wouldn't we imagine, given the prevalence of neurodiversity, that God's own self would be reflected in those who have these diagnoses?

While the reinterpretation of the story of the family from Bethany was originally, of course, a creative speculation for the sake of fulfilling the requirements put forth by my institution for my doctoral degree, I do believe there is power in the narrative as reimagined to see biblical characters in a new and neurodiverse light. Did Mary or Martha or

---

2. Eiesland, *The Disabled God: Toward a Liberatory Theology of Disability.*

Reimagination and neurodivergent possibility

Lazarus ever ask themselves, "Why am I like this?" Who's to say? However, whether they were living with ADHD or not, I think it might be safe to assume they did. For most, this self-reflective question can lead us to deeper introspection and better understanding of our own behaviors, beliefs, and actions.

For others of us, however, it is a constant, nagging, self-deprecating query that does little else than tip the first mental domino over, until we find ourselves in a deep pit of self-loathing. At worst we end up convincing ourselves that we probably misheard our call to ministry, are not cut out for this vocation, and that it would be better if we left to go do literally anything else with our pathetic little lives.

This glimpse into how the rejection sensitivity and emotional dysregulation tend to stay on loop in my brain is not shared to garner pity or dig for compliments and reassurance. Rather, it is shared here to provide a true and sobering portrait of what the internal workings of your neurodiverse clergyperson's world might very well look and feel like even though you, the church congregant, or church or denominational leader will not be able to see it or discern that it is happening from the outside. It is for this very reason that it is of the utmost importance that keeping before ourselves that all people are reflections of the Divine, that *Imago Dei*, the image of God is upon us all is so very important. By the time we are ordained we have spent a lifetime hiding our true selves and trying to blend in with the crowd. We have survived elementary, middle, and high school by the skin of our teeth. And the effort we put into completing our undergraduate and master's level degrees so that we can have even a hope of entering ministry in our beloved, yet rigorous mainline protestant denominations have worn us out before we've even preached our first sermon.

The variety of lenses from which we choose to read scripture, continues to expand. It is my hope that this neurodiversity lens becomes another liberation theology. Joining those of African American, Feminist, Womanist, Latin American and Queer liberation theologies. For, as Eiesland says, "the presence of the disabled God makes it possible to bear a nonconventional body,"[3] and, in this case, noncon-

---

3. Ibid.

ventional mind. And the presence of this framework "enables both a struggle for justice among people with disabilities and an end to estrangement from our own bodies,"[4] and minds.

---

4. Ibid.

6. Ministry in the Margins
Findings on ADHD and clergywomen's vocational realities

While I hate to admit it, the dissertation project upon which this work is built came perilously close to remaining incomplete. It mirrored my ordination process. Completing the writing in a timely fashion was compressed and stressful. This was due to a variety of factors; as someone who is VAST my brain tends to need a certain amount of urgency to complete tasks. My relationship with time, however, has only two settings, "NOW," and "NOT NOW." With a spring deadline for the final draft and consultation with my advisors still months away, the fall and winter months were spent mostly conceptualizing the idea of writing an entire dissertation. Little actual progress was made other than drafting an outline and holding a few conversations with my advisor and mentors.

In addition to struggling to overcome my own brain wiring and the constant loop of self-sabotaging internal monologue beating me down every day, things at work were slipping further and further off course. Once again, my supervisor at the time began to pick up on several of my VAST traits and the way they were presenting. Once again, my natural traits were misunderstood and misinterpreted. None of them were, as far as I could tell, prohibitive of my performing my job or meeting the expectations of my job description. And I was diligently working with a myriad of care providers to manage my VAST traits and regulate myself: my primary care physician (PCP) and mental health nurse practitioner (MHNP) were working together to help me figure out a new medication regimen.

Meanwhile, I was meeting regularly with a therapist as well as a spiritual director and had recently added a clergy coach just for good measure. The tackling of a project in which I had essentially been peeling back my own layers of hurt and confusion, relief, grief, anger, and curiosity about how VAST has affected my life was no small undertaking. Most days I felt as though I was an open, gaping flesh wound walking around.

While I was trying to "keep it together" internally while riding the undulating waves of emotion as I worked through medication shifts and therapy, I also sifted through ten qualitative interview transcripts from women much like myself recounting their own stories of pain and confusion and ponderings about leaving the ministry. Simultaneously, there was also a tidal wave of horrors happening externally at a macro level both locally and globally. A new administration had just been inaugurated and within weeks, the system of checks and balances that once seemed to hold our country together was being dismantled, leaving many people I know, and love, frightened for their well-being and safety.

I was also watching in dismay as national safeguards such as the ADA were coming under attack. That one felt especially personal as less than five years had passed since I had first realized I was someone who could benefit from ADA protection myself. Not to mention the fact that I was also continuously in touch with friends in Ukraine, where I had served years before as a young adult missionary through the United Methodist Church. I was battling daily feelings of helplessness and inadequacy while watching their country be bombed and my own government debate betraying our allies. All of this, when paired with the emotional dysregulation of VAST was soul crushing, to say the least.

As all of this was going on and I was fighting tooth-and-nail to stay mentally, physically, emotionally, and spiritually afloat, my supervisor began a campaign, intentionally or not, to assure me of my inadequacy.

Stemming from one or two minor miscommunications the previous fall, our communication broke down to the point that at the beginning of the second semester (we are both campus pastors) we had to bring in a mediator to work with us. I spent several meetings in a row being told that I wasn't communicating enough, or in the correct ways. This was confounding and infuriating as I had tried both oral and written communication at different points throughout the year only to be met consistently with a misaligned recounting of what had been agreed.

For months I attempted to name continual confusion surrounding one of my job responsibilities. Despite requests for clarity and a clear checklist of tasks to perform, I was never provided one. This did not prevent me from being told every few weeks that I clearly wasn't doing enough. And the *piece de resistance* was when a piece of medical information I had shared in confidence regarding my ongoing medication trials and dosage adjustments—in an attempt to help my colleague better understand some of what I was navigating during a particularly contentious time—was shared publicly during a staff meeting. A clear HIPPA violation.

For a month or more, the crushing sense of rejection from someone I considered not only a close colleague and talented supervisor, but also a friend and mentor was overwhelming. As the weeks wore on, I began to notice my anxiety and depression increasing, making it harder to focus on my various responsibilities. As I was now less than two months away from finishing my degree which was four years in the making, I finally decided I needed to ask for some help. I reached out to my colleagues asking if any of them would be willing to temporarily cover some of my ministry duties, clearly stating my VAST need to hyperfocus for a few writing days. This was so I could complete my dissertation and thus degree, freeing my time up as opposed to risking having the project linger any longer.

When I finally garnered the courage to make the request I was told it was unfair and extreme. Essentially, my appeal was for workplace accommodation for a temporary window of time. I was presented with the option to either take unpaid days or to push my graduation back by an entire year. There did not seem to be any interest from my ministry context to try to understand my VAST needs. Nor was there any attempt to provide reasonable accommodation despite my newfound ability to articulate my needs.

In reflection, I realize I once again became a hollow shell of a person, questioning whether I am even cut out for ministry as a vocation. It was disheartening as this pattern seems to continue to repeat in a variety of ministry contexts.[1] As researchers at the Boston University Anna Howard Shaw Center assert, "the ability to live fully and authentically is crucial for a healthy clergyperson."[2] And instead of living fully and authentically I was trying to hide once again who I truly am in an attempt to keep the peace. Only this time, I realized that was what was happening because now I know myself more fully. I now know that I am someone who must work to find a balance between living with the realities of VAST and my ability to thrive in ministry.

Around this time, I began to feel an impending sense of dread each time I thought about needing to make an appearance at the campus ministry house. And on the days I went in to work there was always some comment or observation made by my supervisor about something I would do or say, or wouldn't do, or I was perceived as *not* saying. All these combined factors drove me further and further away from being able to focus on completing my dissertation. And that is to say nothing of the fact that I no longer felt psychologically safe at work.

I eventually worked with my supervisor to find a creative solution that allowed me, for the following month, and the month that the project was due, to work remotely. For the first time in my professional career, I thought I had finally found a way to creatively and resourcefully readjust my work habits. At least for a short time I was able to stay on staff instead of quitting in disgust and frustration which had, unfortunately, been my professional pattern up to that point. The amount of post-traumatic growth I was seeing and feeling in myself felt like a win in and of itself, whether this project was going to be finished on time or not. And it continued to feel like a win even after

---

1. Horan, "Feminized Servanthood, Gendered Scapegoating, and the Disappearance of Gen-X/Millennial Protestant Clergy Women."
2. Collier, "United Methodist Clergywomen Retention Study."

that ministry setting still found it fit to relieve me of my duties with very little explanation, zero severance, and no transition time or ability to have a "good goodbye" with my students. Once again I had to use copious amounts of mental and emotional energy to avoid spiraling into despair and self-doubt.

As emotionally and spiritually heavy as it could be to be sifting through the transcripts of my peers who experienced similar challenges in their own lives and ministries, I also found reassurance and solace there. I was reminded day in and day out that I am not alone in feeling the stress of trying to manage VAST as a pastor. There are a million and one ways that VAST affects every aspect of our lives, both personal and professional. And we all have stories of feeling misunderstood by our congregations, colleagues, and the leaders to whom we are expected to turn when we need help. There is not a VAST clergywoman I know who does not have at least one tale like the one I was living. Stories of abrupt dismissals and ministry "failures" and forced leaves of absence abound.

While every interviewee's story was moving, none put the need for this work in such sharp relief as Pastor Brook's story of realizing how being VAST had affected her own spiritual wellbeing and sense of self over time. She started by sharing that yes, she does believe that ADHD has affected her spiritual health and admitted that, although she had a planned sabbatical coming up, the elders (governing board) at her church could tell that she was in desperate need of a break much sooner than that.

As she shared, we both grieved at the weight of the realization of the detrimental effect ADHD has had on her spiritual wellbeing over time, as well as the beauty, love, and care shown by her congregation. By the end of her sharing, we sat amazed at the peace brought to her by the Spirit during the retreat her congregation gifted to her.

She began recounting how she had been experiencing more struggles than usual due to a medication shortage and the fact that she had been forced off of her ADHD medication for about a month. The focus that was already hard to come by was feeling nearly impossible. She reflected:

Findings on ADHD and clergywomen's vocational realities

I just thought, *"You know, they're sending me on this spiritual retreat and, like, what? What the heck am I even gonna do? What am I gonna do? I'm just gonna go somewhere, and I'm gonna, like, binge Netflix the whole time, or I'm gonna do the things I'm not supposed to do. You know, I'm not... I don't have meds, and I cannot... There's no way I can focus to get anything out of the spiritual retreat. And it's... it's just me like this."*

Unsure of how the retreat would go, Pastor Brook accepted the gift of time and the use of a congregation member's cabin. She packed several books, despite not being sure if or how she would be able to use them:

Anyway, I ended up going... I took a bunch of books, and I was like, *"I don't even know what I'm going to do with this. I'm just going to take these books, and we'll see where we go."*

Once settled in at the cabin, Pastor Brook let the retreat unfold and found that what she had though of as a lack-of-focus due to her ADHD was actually a profound gift that allowed her to follow the prompting of the Spirit in new and life-giving ways:

And so... I get there, and the next morning I woke up. I'm in this lake house, and I like, get out on the porch... and I just take my Bible and a couple of devotionals, and I just kinda... just randomly start jumping in and I start reading. And I had a journal. And what I did was I read a little bit of the devotional, and then when I hit a Scripture that they started referring to I'd jump over to the Bible and take a look at that Scripture, and then maybe I'd read the study notes for the Scripture, and then I would go back to the devotional, and I would jot down all the things that I felt like jumped out to me as I was going in my notebook without any agenda, just jotting them down.

Soon enough it wasn't just the unstructured exploring of scripture, reading, and journaling that seemed to benefit from Pastor Brook's

ADHD. She quickly found herself more engaged and connected to God's creation:

> And I'm sitting outside. And at some point, you know, there was a crane on the water. And so, I kind of like, watched the crane for however long, and then got back to what I was doing, and then I… there were these chipmunks chasing each other. At one point I went and, stood at the edge of the… the deck and watched the chipmunks. And you know this was like 20 minutes. I think that I saw a beaver at one point.

Pastor Brook recalled how that entire day played out and allowed her to begin to see her ADHD in a new light:

> So, anyway, this is just how the entire day went, and just reading, moving to the Bible when I wanted to. Moving back to, you know, just back and forth, stopping and looking around me. And when I got back from the retreat the thing I just kept reflecting on was, *"I think that I have always seen my ADHD as, like, a hindrance to my spiritual life, because, as a pastor, there are all these expectations on you that you are 'supposed' to do the things, right?"* You're supposed to… supposed to be "good at prayer." You're supposed to be "good at meditation" and all the things. And… I'm not, I'm really, just truly, like, those aren't my things, and it… and it's hard to be able to admit that because [the internal thoughts] are like, "How do you? How can you even be a pastor? If you can't, you know, you can't do those things? That's like, pretty basic right?"

Pastor Brook recounted prior retreats and programs which she had participated in that never felt quite like they were right for truly nourishing her own spirituality and spiritual wellbeing:

> And I've been on so many spiritual retreats. I did the programs I was supposed to do. I was in this program for new pastors, and they would take us for this weeklong retreat. And you know, we

had a day of silence which never went well for me. Never! I never knew what the heck to do with a day of silence. And, you know, I've been to the workshops. It's the self-care thing, like, I've done all that. But nothing like, really felt like it could fix it. And so then, a lot of times, I feel like I'm just, again, just masking or just playing, like I don't know. Cos-playing as a pastor, because they're the things that I'm supposed to be able to do.

Something about this unstructured retreat time, gifted to her by her own congregation, unlocked a new understanding of how her ADHD, particularly the trait of inattention, could actually be something that brought her closer to God:

> I feel like I'm just... just masking or just playing... I don't know... Cos-playing as a pastor.
> -*Pastor Brook*

And that's why I thought I had to have the meds, like, there was no way I could get anything out of [this retreat] unless I had meds that could make me focus right? Focus on contemplative prayer or focus on what I was reading. But the reality is, what actually helped me come away feeling more spiritually nourished... was the inattention, right? It was the ability to... to be reading something and have my... have the thought pop in my head and immediately go look something up and then finish that thought, and then go back and then you know, whatever. Or just to stop what I was doing to watch an animal because, like there was no... I wasn't accountable to anyone. There was no timeline, no agenda. It was gonna be what it was gonna be. And then, you know, whenever I was done, it was okay to be done.

And an added benefit of the time away was that it also fed Pastor Brook's ability to think creatively for her congregation and in her ministry:

There were several, like, big ideas that emerged, and what I was reading [on the retreat] then really carried through to some stuff I was doing at the church. Then I think it showed up. Sermons, and I think it showed up in just some other random things, and… I can't do that here. That's not what this job is like, day in and day out. That is not what this job is. This job is being an executive director of a spiritually based nonprofit that does, you know, does all the things, right? And I have wonderful lay leaders. But at the end of the day, the things… the things do fall to me. And so, the ability to just take a day. And just because here, even if I did it, like, even if I had the discipline to be able to do it, I don't think that I could. I would always be thinking about that other thing I 'needed' to be doing, and I couldn't just be in the moment.

What a gift to be able to realize that one's ADHD might actually be the very gift needed to succeed in both personal and professional spiritual life:

But I realized that, yeah, I… that while I thought that my ADHD was the thing that was keeping me from being close to God it was not allowing me to be fully myself and to live into that ADHD. That was actually, like, the barrier there. I'm… I'm honestly super grateful to have had that experience to carry it with me into my Sabbatical.

Brook was far from alone in sharing how her VAST traits have affected her self-perception and spiritual wellbeing. Every single one of the ten clergywomen I spoke with had a story or an example of a time that they felt they weren't good enough or holy enough or disciplined enough to be a pastor. Fortunately, like Brook, many of them are beginning to see how being VAST is, as Brook says, not a barrier from God, but rather a gift from God. Imagine how much healthier and happier VAST clergy could be if they had the benefit of external affirmation from understanding and supportive congregations and colleagues as they worked to see themselves as spiritually gifted.

7. The Intersection of ADHD and Ministry
Toward a fuller understanding of VAST in clergywomen

In these final chapters we will explore the ways in which eight of the most common traits of VAST are likely to be noticed by others and thus affect the ministry of clergywomen. These traits are Inattention, Hyperactivity, Impulsivity, Rejection Sensitivity, Emotional Dysregulation, Hyperfocus, Timeblindness, and Divergent Thinking. Here in Chapter 7, we will explore how these traits have shown up in ministry and how they can be both gifts and challenges for clergywomen. In Chapter 8 we will explore how each trait can be better supported by churches and denominational leaders to help VAST clergywomen thrive in ministry.

Inattention

Inattention is perhaps my "favorite" trait to explore now that I know that my VAST diagnosis is "ADHD—Inattentive Subtype," which was something I had never heard of before. However, since I learned this and started reading about the condition and how it presents, especially in girls and women, it's a wonder to me that no adult in my life growing up ever thought something might be amiss. Perhaps this is because, like Pastor Nicole shares, "Like many people with ADHD, I think, especially women, I am fairly good at masking things."[1] Inattention makes sitting through meetings especially difficult as Pastor Fiona shares, "That's my biggest problem. I can get easily distracted during meetings and I'll just, like, look around the room."[2] Same, girl, same.

Inattention also has a huge effect on neurodiverse clergywomen's abilities to fulfill certain pastoral responsibilities, namely, pastoral care and visitation duties. Six out of ten of the women I interviewed named pastoral care as a major challenge in ministry. For some it was that regular visitation simply does not seem urgent enough or interesting enough to hold their attention. It's too easy to say, "If I'm not interested in something, then 'I'll do it later,'"[3] but due to the challenges of object permanence, later rarely ever comes, especially when it comes to those church members who are not urgently needing care but are also not able to come to church regularly because they are homebound. As one pastor stated, for these individuals it is not that we do not care about them as their pastors, but, unfortunately, it's simply that, "Oops, 'I forgot that you existed,' to quote the indomitable Taylor Swift. And that's actually a big thing that [due to my trait of inattention] I forgot you existed. I kind of say it as a joke, but that out of sight out of mind thing."[4]

For others, the lack of motivation to attend to pastoral care calls stems from the lack of dopamine and interest these tasks hold. Pastor Elizabeth, who would rather do almost anything else, puts it this way, "Okay. I... I hate small talk. Please don't make me go on any more in person visits. I'll do the ones I have to. I'm amazing at the crisis ones— you call me to the hospital for a crisis? I am looking fantastic. But sitting listening to the same little old lady with dementia tell me the same ten stories? I can't do it. Horrible!"[5]

Finally, our trait of inattention makes completing annual reports and attending denominational meetings, of which all of us are required to attend at least annually, feats of super-human endurance. Pastor

---

1. Nicole, "005.Nicole."
2. Fiona, "003.Fiona."
3. Ruby, "001.Ruby."
4. Fiona, "003.Fiona."
5. Elizabeth, "002.Elizabeth."

Nicole shares, "Diocesan convention is like literal torture for me... I have to bring, like, a whole bag of snacks and various forms of hydration and activities to be able to reasonably get through."[6]

Hyperactivity

There's a familiar object lesson using the image of a duck on water to illustrate how someone's mind works when they are stressed or trying to pull off a big event. You know, where someone says, "If you look at a duck on the water it looks like it's gliding effortlessly across the surface of the water, but in reality, it's feet are under the water paddling like crazy." This provides a general understanding of this next VAST trait and its effect on your beloved clergywoman.

Our minds, by and large, are going at a warp speed. All the time. And it is *exhausting*, often leading to, at the least, mental overwhelm and at the worst to burnout. Pastor Nicole shares, "Hyperactive brain. Yes. The, like, inability to shut off the thoughts means I think I spend a lot more time thinking about work than I mean to... I think that leads me to kind of paths of burnout more quickly."[7] While Pastor Louise says, "I have a bazillion ideas a day, and they all go on my list, and then I'm routinely stressed out all the time - only by a list of my own making."[8] And, as Pastor Elizabeth shares, sometimes the draining nature of the internal work going on in our minds stalls our outward productivity. "Sometimes I have a hard time getting started into projects because that brain is going. How can this go wrong? It's like having a nest of wires in my head, and the impulses are going twice as fast."[9]

When we can "get out of our heads" for a moment the trait of hyperactivity can then have effects on our communication. Pastor Fiona shares, "One of the ways I think [hyperactivity] shows up is if I get excited about something I'm preaching, I will talk faster, and my pitch changes," so she compensates, "I write out my sermons to keep

6. Nicole, "005.Nicole."
7. Ibid.
8. Louise, "008.Louise."
9. Elizabeth, "002.Elizabeth."

myself from going on too many tangents. There are still tangents sometimes, but it gives me a center point to come back to."[10]

To a lesser degree, at least for the women who participated in this research, hyperactivity can also be manifested physically. This can be as simple as our leg bouncing during a meeting or more noticeable such as needing to stand up at the back of longer meetings to keep ourselves engaged. Whether it is observed by anyone else, the physical manifestation of hyperactivity can be a cause of stress or shame, especially if we perceive it to be noticeable and a point of judgement from our congregations. Pastor Elizabeth explains how she noticed how her physical hyperactivity was becoming more visible in her worship leadership, "But the hyperactivity physically, I notice by not being behind the pulpit. I now walk. I can't just stand because the pulpit—I used to hold it—and that would hold me in place. I would love that I could catch myself. Now I wander all over the place and I will notice when I'm up front, some of the hyperactivity comes out in certain stims I have. Like—if I'm feeling super anxious—I'll start flicking my fingers at my side and I'll catch it in videos now."[11]

Impulsivity

Rounding out the third and final ADHD trait that's officially listed in the DSM-V is impulsivity. While this trait is generally less prevalent in girls and women than in boys and men with VAST, it still exists and can be one of the most noticeable traits we have. Impulsivity affects our ability to prioritize pastoral tasks and can hinder our ability to follow through. It can also affect our communication and our relationship to financial wellness, both personally and professionally. Pastor Nicole shares, "I will impulsively decide to pursue a new idea and get other people on board with it, and then I have to see it through from there. So that is one that gets me,"[12] as she recounted several projects she was excited to start, but then never seemed to quite bring to

---

10. Fiona, "003.Fiona."
11. Elizabeth, "002.Elizabeth."
12. Nicole, "005.Nicole."

completion. Pastor Fiona faces a similar challenge, "I get really excited about a new project, and then... I'm on to the next shiny thing, and I forget what I was doing."[13]

Several pastors shared that their impulsiveness can be most noticeable in meetings when they either get excited or are afraid they are going to forget what they are planning to say or lose the thought in their mind. This is noticed by others when they blurt things out in meetings or impulsively interrupt others. While not an insurmountable challenge, as with many VAST traits, when it happens, we tend to feel embarrassed and ashamed that we weren't more "professional."

Finally, regarding the implications on financial management, Pastor Gloria shares, "[Impulsivity's] been more of a problem in churches where money is really tight. Because I'm gonna spend the whole budget, and if your expectation is that I'm gonna pace my spending through the year, or that I'm going to spend as little as possible, then we're probably gonna have a problem."[14]

Rejection Sensitivity

We've already touched on how pastoral care tasks are affected by the trait of inattention for several VAST clergywomen. For others that named pastoral care as a challenge, it's a mix of social anxiety tied up in their rejection sensitivity that makes pastoral care feel impossible. Pastor Sophia shares, "I used to think I can't do pastoral care home visits because of social anxiety and fear of going to see other people... And I still cannot get out the door. Like, I cannot leave my house to go.'"[15] And Ruby admits, "I... I want so badly for people to not kick me out of a room, you know? If I'm... if I'm in a hospital room, or, you know, if I'm working with a kid or whatever it's like I... I get deeply, deeply wounded if somebody kicks me out."[16]

Rejection sensitivity has the most effect on VAST pastors' experience of receiving feedback. The way in which VAST clergywomen

---

13. Fiona, "003.Fiona."
14. Gloria, "006.Gloria."
15. Sophia, "004.Sophia."
16. Ruby, "001.Ruby."

experience things like annual reviews is something that bears special mention. Speaking in a way that rings true with my own experience, Pastor Louise states that, "Receiving feedback can feel like a personal attack rather than constructive criticism. I often have to remind myself that it's not about me."[17] Likewise, Pastor Ruby shares that, "When someone criticizes my work, I feel like I'm being rejected as a person, not just my work."[18]

I know for myself that when it is Annual Review time that I am going to need to intentionally block off time on my calendar following the review—good or bad—to tend to myself. No matter what, I know myself well enough now to know that, however the feedback is provided, I will need time to sift through what was said and will need time to detach from my ministry area and colleagues and congregants to rest and recenter after any kind of review.

Sometimes nothing even needs to be said explicitly as the mere idea or sheer perception of rejection will affect our ministries. Pastor Ruby again shares that simply the thought of risking rejection usually launches her into overthinking ministry decisions. The fear that those around her will not approve of what she decides is debilitating. And when this happens, she admits that "I sometimes avoid taking risks in ministry because I'm afraid it will lead to rejection or failure."[19]

Between the fear of rejection, our profound sensitivity to it, and our compromised ability to regulate our emotions, our need for reassurance skyrockets. All too often, clergywomen with VAST spend hours upon hours second-guessing ourselves and wasting untold amounts of mental, spiritual, and emotional energy wondering if our congregations and colleagues approve of us. This can become draining for those around us as well, especially when we are in states of unhealth or during a particularly rocky patch mentally, emotionally, or spiritually. In these seasons we will seek that reassurance *ad nauseum* but are incapable of stopping ourselves despite our awareness that we may be overwhelming others. It is, as they say, a double-edged sword.

---

17. Louise, "008.Louise."
18. Ruby, "001.Ruby."
19. Ibid.

Emotional Dysregulation

One of the clearest signs that I might have had something "going on" in my youth is, in hindsight, clear as day to me. And that would be the emotional dysregulation I have experienced since my earliest days. It's hard to explain to those living outside of your own brain what it is like to know, logically, that your reaction to something—anything—is disproportionate to whatever has taken place. And yet, despite your knowing and your understanding, you are still unable to tone down or regulate your reaction be it joy, or sadness, or anger. It is truly infuriating to want to "calm down," while being rendered essentially defenseless against your own emotions.

For clergy who are told regularly that they are to be the "non-anxious presence" in their congregations and places of employment, this is a surefire recipe for VAST clergywomen to think they are a failure. Emotional dysregulation might be the preeminent VAST trait neurodiverse clergywomen need others to understand. We need those around us to help find creative ways to support our emotional dysregulation, especially as it is the trait that has the biggest negative effect on our self-perception. As Ruby shares, "The expectation to always be a calm and collected leader can be overwhelming when my emotions are all over the place. ... I worry that if I show my emotions, people will see me as weak or incapable."[20]

Not only does our emotional dysregulation wreak havoc on us internally, it can also manifest in ways that are more noticeable to others. Ruby continues, "When I'm emotionally dysregulated, my decision-making becomes impaired, and I struggle to think clearly about what needs to be done... I struggle to connect with my congregants and provide the care that they need."[21]

Pastoral ministry is taxing on pastors' minds, hearts, and souls in ways that few other professions are. For those of us who need to work double - or triple - time to stay regulated, this can take incredible amounts of time and intention to manage. Pastor Louise observed that,

---

20. Ibid.
21. Ibid.

It is truly infuriating to want to "calm down," while being rendered essentially defenseless against your own emotions.
For clergy who are told regularly that they are to be the "non-anxious presence" in their congregations and places of employment, this is a surefire recipe for VAST clergywomen to think they are a failure.

"I have now come to understand that a good 20% to 30% of my week is just processing emotions and space and feelings and vibes and trying to keep the… keep all of this moving and humming and regulated otherwise it's a nightmare."[22]

She continued by sharing this example, "Yesterday, going on a two-hour walk and taking a shower and screaming, like, that's part of [my] pastoral care, and work for [myself] to be able to now, this morning, get up and write a sermon in an hour that I'm ready to give, like, but I had to do all that to get there."[23]

While I still am finding best practices for myself in regard to regulating my emotions, I appreciated hearing the stories of colleagues who are further ahead on the journey of radical self-acceptance. I find it truly inspirational and full of hope that a new future of pastoral care and understanding is coming for clergy.

Hyperfocus

The discussions surrounding how hyperfocus has affected our ministry practice was less laden with the challenges it poses. Instead, it leaned a little more positive as many of us see our ability to hyperfocus as one of the few "superpowers" VAST affords us. Yet it still presents some hurdles.

Many of us find that we can get so absorbed in certain tasks that the rest of the world sort of falls away and it can take extreme effort to bring ourselves back to the present moment. We can also find it difficult to switch our attention to something different after being in a

---

22. Louise, "008.Louise."
23. Ibid.

hyperfocus state. Pastor Gloria puts it this way, "When I go into hyper-focus, I can dive deep into sermon preparation or planning, but it often means I lose track of time and neglect other responsibilities... Some-times I find it hard to shift my focus back to what's important after getting caught up in a hyper focused state."[24]

In the most extreme cases of hyperfocus many of us can forget to take breaks for the simple necessities, as Pastor Nicole shares, "When I'm hyperfocused, I can forget to eat or take breaks, which can lead to burnout."[25] Also challenging can be the way that hyperfocus is perceived by those around us which can sometimes lead to relational strain. Pastor Fiona shares, "My hyperfocus can sometimes make me seem distant or unavailable to my congregants, especially when I'm deeply engaged in a project."[26]

While truly a superpower in many regards, hyperfocus can also have negative effects on our ministry and relationships as neurodi-verse clergywomen. In the next chapter we will envision support strategies to increase clergy retention.

Timeblindness

In perhaps the most comical example of my own VAST tendency to miss details during this project I originally neglected to include "Time-blindness" as a trait to ask my participants about. Even though time-blindness was my own most noticeable and concerning challenge at the time, not to mention that it is among the most outwardly noticeable VAST traits to others, I still somehow managed to forget to explore timeblindness with my interview participants!

It wasn't until I was in the middle of one of the interviews that I realized my oversight. I also only noticed because one of my eagle-eyed participants noticed and mentioned being surprised that I hadn't asked about timeblindness. Therefore, the responses to this question came in written form after the initial interviews were completed.

---

24. Gloria, "006.Gloria."
25. Nicole, "005.Nicole."
26. Fiona, "003.Fiona."

Toward a fuller understanding of VAST in clergywomen

One of the major ways in which timeblindness affects the ministry of VAST clergywomen is that we tend to have an unrealistic optimism regarding how much we can reasonably get done in any given day. We are either consistently over- or underestimating how much time a task is going to take. Pastor Nicole puts it this way, "Timeblindness is a struggle in ministry because I have a tough time understanding how long something actually will take me to complete, which can lead to me feeling underprepared or rushed."[27] Similarly, Pastor Sophia shares, "I also way overestimate how much I can get done in a given period."[28]

In addition to the daily challenges of time management and task prioritization, timeblindness can affect long term projects and responsibilities. This can lead to inadvertent procrastination on more important tasks, especially if the tasks we would rather spend time on hold more interest for us and our dopamine-seeking brains. Pastor Louise recounts that, "I frequently believe I can get more tasks done than the amount of time I have allotted. I struggle with time management because I'll prioritize something that appears urgent to me but later, it turns out it was just my brain assigning equal urgency to everything."[29]

Finally, as with almost every VAST trait we have explored, our timeblindness can have negative effects on our relationships both personally and professionally. As Pastor Nicole shares:

It's also a challenge when I'm running late and such, because people perceive it as something negative, like irresponsibility or lack of care.

If someone tells me they need me to do a thing, I need a deadline, and gentle reminders really help make sure that I can see that deadline approaching. And yes, I can do that on my own, and I'm getting better at systematizing those processes, but it's a work in progress. I think a general understanding of

---

27. Nicole, "005.Nicole."
28. Sophia, "004.Sophia."
29. Louise, "008.Louise."

the ADHD brain having a "NOW" and a "NOT NOW" setting can be helpful for people I work closely with as well. If someone tells me they need something from me today, I'm probably going to manage to do that, because it translates as "NOW," but if they say they need me to do something by the end of next week, that is "NOT NOW", and my brain will just put it in a box and forget to get it out.[30]

Divergent Thinking

The eighth and final trait of VAST that I chose to explore in-depth with my research participants was what I chose to call "Divergent Thinking." That is, thinking that VAST brains seem to be able to do effortlessly and can strike others as incredibly creative or "out-of-the-box." Similarly to hyperfocus, this trait appears to err on the side of ministry superpower but does take some time to learn how to harness, manage, and direct for the most effective leadership and greatest ministry wins.

It is the Divergent Thinking of clergywomen with VAST that lead churches to try new things such as wear birthday party hats and have a reception with cake and punch on their church's founding anniversary or.... Birthday.[31] It is also what led one pastor to work with a local non-profit agency to address the housing crisis in their area, leading their church to see the need and guide them to the point of using their resource of extra land to provide the space for new homes to be built in their community. So much good, faithful, and creative ministry happens when VAST clergywomen are encouraged and affirmed in their creativity and are given the support, resources, and help they need to attain what once seemed impossible.

On the flip side of this, some reigning in by the community is often in order. As Pastor Marley shared, "I've had some wild [ideas]. And then, like, you know, there's certain [reminders] like, 'Hey, can you be... Remember, remember, this carpet is brand new [from my congre-

---

30. Nicole, "005.Nicole."
31. Marley, "007.Marley."

gational leaders]."[32] VAST clergywomen by and large appreciate their lay people helping them prioritize and decide what great ideas to act on and which ones to set aside for a time to return to later once the initial excitement (and, emotional dysregulation, perhaps?) has had a chance to subside.

With a little conversation and compromise though, the sky's the limit for churches with a willing heart, the capacity to be flexible, and the gift of a VAST pastor at the helm to help them imagine new and creative ways to follow the Spirit's leading both within their church and out in their communities.

---

32. Ibid.

8. Toward a Faithful Response

Recommendations for supporting neurodivergent clergywomen

We have now thoroughly explored the WHY behind the need for local churches and denominational church leaders to improve their understanding of neurodiverse clergywomen. We have also discussed WHO needs to make that effort and those changes. Now, let us turn our attention finally to the HOW of creating better support systems for neurodiverse clergywomen.

As a reminder, the WHY of this need is first and foremost to improve the health and well-being of these incredible and VAST clergywomen. By doing so we will improve clergy retention—as we learned that clergywomen leave ministry at a rate ten percent higher than that of their male colleagues.[1] The WHO includes members of the congregations who receive, by either appointment or call, VAST clergywomen, but especially the lead team members of Administrative Councils, Vestries, Sessions, and governing boards. Denominational leaders tasked with supporting local churches and clergy within their assigned regions bear the bulk of responsibility to educate themselves and provide the right education and training for church boards. This

---

1. Collier, "United Methodist Clergywomen Retention Study."

will help them to be prepared to receive these gifted clergy and to set up all parties for success.

As with almost any topic or issue of concern within the church the following recommendations will feel both too easy as well as nearly impossible to implement. At the root of the matter, what VAST clergy-women desire is for our churches and church leaders "to really under-stand the absolute gift that they have in an ADHD-brained pastor."[2]

If we are left consistently fighting the stigma and misunderstanding of our condition rather than working together with our churches to find more collaborative and grace-full modes of operating with one another, then there will be neither change nor growth. We'll be left with only a repetition of the unhealthy patterns that have led so many of us to contemplate leaving ministry all together.[3] This also harkens back to the story of the gentlemen on the train in India that I shared at the outset. While in Western cultures individuals with ADHD/VAST and other neurodiverse traits are seen as having a "disability," other cultures understand us as "old souls." What a change waiting to happen when our spiritual giftedness via our God-created brain circuitry is recognized rather than shunned as faith leaders!

In the previous chapter, we explored eight of the common traits of VAST that are most likely to be noticed by others. They can be noticed even if members or leaders do not know that the clergywoman presenting these traits has a diagnosis. Disclosing a diagnosis such as VAST still holds a lot of trepidation for many of us precisely because of the stigma we know still surrounds it. Fortunately, the tips, tricks, insights, and recommendations made here are ones that will not only benefit VAST clergywomen, but in fact benefit all clergy and laity.

> It is imperative to respect healthy boundaries set by your clergy person, extend grace, and approach one another with curiosity rather than judgment or assumptions.

Most of the advice that we are about to share can truly be boiled

---

2. Louise, "008.Louise."

3. Horan, "Feminized Servanthood, Gendered Scapegoating, and the Disappearance of Gen-X/Millennial Protestant Clergy Women."

down into a few simple things: trying things differently, being flexible, and assuming the best intent. Additionally, it is imperative to respect healthy boundaries set by your clergyperson, extend grace, and approach one another with curiosity rather than judgement and assumptions. Finally, investing the time and energy to educate yourselves about VAST so the weight of helping you understand does not fall upon the VAST person themselves. And of course, returning to the basics: showing each other simple respect would go a long, long way to improve the relationship between VAST clergywomen and their congregations and their denominational leaders. Please read on for more detailed insights and recommendations.

Inattention

Traits of inattention prove the most challenging for clergywomen in two primary ways. First, as we discovered, it makes sitting through meetings, especially long denominational meetings and conferences that are often required incredibly difficult. Secondly, inattention can lead us to either procrastinate or forget to complete certain tasks on our to-do lists entirely, especially if they are further out on our calendars, when our timeblindness might also become a factor.

To help with this, we would love to see our denominational leaders "scheduling meetings in shorter bursts and putting in breaks…. Being able to break things down into smaller sessions for folks, create space to tackle one thing at a time, that would be helpful."[4] Normalizing people being allowed to get up and stand at the back of the meeting space, no questions asked, or encouraging people to get up, go to the restroom, or bring snacks or water to keep hydrated through longer sessions would also be worthwhile.

Closer to home our local churches and ministry contexts need to be "moving towards more collaborative approaches to ministry."[5] A great deal of clergy burnout can be attributed to clergy feeling overworked and under supported. In the case of pastoral care, which we have

---

4. Nicole, "005.Nicole."
5. Sophia, "004.Sophia."

discovered is an area of immense challenge for a majority of VAST clergywomen, it would be incredibly helpful for our ministry partners and leadership team to "hold us accountable in kindness, with kindness and love... instead of judging the ways that our minds are different, try to understand it and think about how they can support it."[6] This could look like someone helping to schedule visits for the pastor, gently reminding the pastor to make their monthly visitations and creating a sense of urgency, or even launching a lay visitation team so that the work of visitation is delegated and does not rest solely on the pastor's shoulders.

Finally, it is imperative that churches provide both clear expectations and firm deadlines for important events and needs. As Pastor Gloria states, "Some churches know damn well what they want. They just won't tell you out loud, you know?" She astutely asks, "Don't you know all you're doing is inadvertently creating tests that your pastor will fail?"[7] For VAST pastors who have the trait of inattention, when we have too much to attend to some things naturally start to fall off our radar. This is not because we don't care about them, but because our attention is focused elsewhere and we lack the amount of executive function needed to regulate and direct it. Therefore, it is highly unlikely that we will be able to make correct educated guesses about what our congregations want or expect from us. Under this system of operation we are, intentionally or not, set up for failure from the get go.

Hyperactivity

While I cannot speak for all VAST clergywomen I can tell you that, for myself, it is the mental hyperactivity that I find the most draining about being VAST. At all times there are the equivalent of 50 or more open tabs in my brain. I'm never quite sure which one I'm supposed to be looking at or focusing on. They all seem equally important to me. Then, every third hour or so, the little jellybean guys from my long-

---

6. Fiona, "003.Fiona."
7. Gloria, "006.Gloria."

term memory (Inside Out reference. Please stop reading and go watch that movie if you didn't catch it. I'll wait...) decide to send that "Double Mint Gum" jingle back to headquarters and I find myself distracted and off task for the 214th time that day. Most of the women in this study shared that their hyperactivity primarily shows up within their own minds as racing thoughts. However, hyperactivity can also present physically, and we will address both.

Pastor Louise, who experiences hyperactivity more internally, was direct and to the point when she shared, "I think [hyperactivity] is really hard for me. That one's not a fun superpower. It's really over-whelming inside. I think a lot of that emotional work would just be such a gift for me to be in spaces as a pastor and feel that who I fully am is understood and loved. But also, just for people to understand this is a disability that you're working with here. And that's really hard."[8]

Having church leaders come alongside us, at both the local and denominational levels, ready to help us prioritize our ministry goals and help us come up with a do-able, bite-size, to-do list would be incredibly beneficial. Or ensuring that VAST coaches are a covered service through denominational health plans would be a dream.

For pastors whose hyperactivity may be more noticeable to outsiders because it shows up in our bodies, it would be helpful for churches to normalize, validate, and empathize with us. Turning a blind eye to bouncing knees or tapping feet in meetings and not drawing attention to the fact that we might be clicking our pens more than you would ideally like can be a small thing that makes a big difference in ensuring we do not feel shamed about this release of pent-up energy.

If your VAST clergywoman is often coloring, doodling, or working on a knitting, crocheting, or needlepoint project in meetings or long conference sessions, please don't assume that she isn't paying atten-tion. Keeping her hands busy might be the very thing that allows her to engage fully in the session because the work of her hands is helping quiet her brain enough to focus. Likewise, don't assume that someone

---

8. Louise, "008.Louise."

choosing to stand at the back of the presentation hall or choosing to go on a walk during the lunch session instead of networking indicates anti-social tendencies or disinterest. Chances are that we're doing everything we can to stay engaged. And trying to do so in a way that is the least disruptive to everyone else.

Churches also need to be prepared to meet the needs of their VAST clergywomen physically, both in the office and in their home if they are living in church-owned housing. When she asks for a standing desk or informs you that the air conditioning unit is too loud and prevents her from concentrating and being able to get work done, please believe her. And fix it. Do not leave your gifted, VAST clergywomen to suffer something because you think "it's no big deal," when in fact it could be the last straw that leads your talented and VAST clergyperson to start interviewing for jobs in other sectors far, far outside the church.

Impulsivity

Impulsivity is one of the most shame-inducing traits of VAST for many women.

This is the trait that is most likely to wreak havoc on our finances and our relationships. Pastor Louise recommends that our church leadership teams would be well advised to be prepared to be the "guardrails,"[9] that can help hone us in and help us refocus. Often, we impulsively try to go in too many directions all at once, or the great idea we have needs funding and instead of waiting for the committee decisions, we're prone to decide we'd rather beg for forgiveness than ask for permission. This can get us in trouble and jeopardize our relationships with our congregants and leaders.

Our impulsiveness can also inhibit our ability to think before we speak. We are more likely to blurt out the thoughts in our heads instead of filtering them and tend to interrupt in meetings or in conversations. Often our interruptions are due to our own excitement and readiness to either try and learn more by asking a question, or to try and connect by sharing a thought or story of our own to prove to you

---

9. Ibid.

that we are listening and have gone through something similar. Unfortunately, this can come across as rude in a variety of ways. Once again, education and training for leadership teams to help them understand this natural tendency in those with VAST would go a long way to hopefully help our congregations and leaders be better prepared to experience this and to embrace it as part of who we are rather than resent it due to misunderstanding.

Now, impulsivity can also have the effect of helping certain clergy-women be more "fun, gregarious, happy, engaging kind of pastor(s)."[10] Validating and embracing us as we truly are so we can feel safe to be our whole selves is a gift beyond measure. When we feel safe enough to "unmask" and live authentically as ourselves, everyone benefits. It can improve not only our overall mood and wellbeing but can also become a strength in the pulpit and in other areas of our ministry. As Pastor Marley shares, "I think when I stepped into the pulpit, fully embracing who I was, not only as a queer woman, but also as a person who wanted to make a side comment, and not just like, fully reading my manuscript, exactly like when I allowed that a little bit of impulsivity in the preaching, a little bit of, like, 'I need to say, I just need to go on this sidetrack,' people were like, 'You are 'So You,' when you preach,' and, like, isn't that one of the goals of preaching?"[11]

Rejection Sensitivity

Hopefully at this point we have begun to make some connections for those of you reading this book that are helping you see and perceive your VAST clergywomen in a new and gentler light. My prayer is that you are already beginning to see the areas in which the actions of your pastor, now that you know she is VAST, might be making more sense to you. Please hold on to this new knowledge and understanding as we turn our attention now to how to best understand, accommodate, and support clergywomen who live with rejection sensitivity dysphoria and emotional dysregulation.

---

10. Fiona, "003.Fiona."
11. Marley, "007.Marley."

Recommendations for supporting neurodivergent clergywomen

Please keep before you that we are talking about what is still classi-fied as a true disability. The outsized reactions and disproportionate emotions are very likely truly out of the full control of your VAST cler-gyperson. It is going to take empathy, understanding, and support to help them achieve success in their ministries which, as with all of these recommendations, only stand to improve the relationship between your church and your pastor. The overall quality of ministry you all will be able to do together moving forward with understanding, grace, and a commitment to transparent communication and unconditional support.

First and foremost, congregations must start training their leadership teams and members on the futility of sharing every complaint and gripe

> "Churches tend to be the most toxic places for conversation."
> - *Pastor Gloria*

directly with their VAST pastor. Pastor Gloria rightly observes that simply "being mindful of how we speak to, and with, one another would be a huge improvement. Churches tend to be the most toxic places for conversation. Which, you know, is antithetical to what we should be... If your hope is to have a pastor who's invested in you and in the future of your church, maybe treat that person the way you would want somebody to respect you, you know?"[12]

Pastor Nicole coaches, "don't tell your clergy every single thing you dislike about whatever they did. Hold it in. If there's 1) nothing that can be done about it, we don't need to know and it's not helpful for us. 2) If it's not something that you are willing to help with, I don't need to know. I don't need to know. You don't need to tell me the thing that you didn't like about how I did whatever if you are not following that up with, *'How can I help do it differently next time?'* or something along those lines."[13]

Given that not every congregant is going to agree to take such training or attend a workshop, it is likely that, despite our best efforts, these comments are going to continue. However, it would be a great gift if, over time, their frequency noticeably declined. One of the ways

---

12. Gloria, "006.Gloria."
13. Nicole, "005.Nicole."

church leadership teams can balance the scales on feedback from the deluge of negative comments we often hear is to take utmost care in preparing and delivering annual reviews and having conversations with their neurodiverse clergyperson as leaders in the church.

The tried and true "compliment sandwich" is a great place to start. All too often the annual reviews clergy receive feel more like hatchet jobs than constructive times of mutual sharing and it sure doesn't feel like we're on the same team working toward a mutual goal of caring for our communities. Please, please, for the love of God, make sure there is a 2-to-1 ratio of positive feedback for your VAST clergyperson and not simply a list of all their faults. I promise you the only thing that you will do is stab a hole through their heart and send them into a weeks-long internal battle that will be draining not only for them, but for their support systems.

As sure as the sun will rise tomorrow, after any review your VAST clergyperson will need to process what they were told and will begin to seek validation and reassurance from multiple sources. In the worst-case scenarios, a disproportionately negative review can trigger the often-associated anxiety and depression in your VAST clergyperson. Often this results in their shutting down and pulling away from your community. All of this can be easily avoided simply by having leaders trained and equipped in providing constructive feedback and ensuring that all annual reviews are balanced and fair.

Relationships are, of course, in need of mutuality and reciprocity, so there is also an onus on VAST clergy themselves to ensure that they have their own support systems in place. Denominations need to be sure that mental health services such as therapy and medical providers are adequately covered as are prescription drug plans for those who use medication as a part of their VAST management plan. Receiving feedback and navigating human-to-human relationships is a part of life and necessary for the work we do as clergy. If everyone does their part to ensure proper support and fair assessment of VAST clergy-women, we'll all benefit.

Emotional Dysregulation

A close cousin to rejection sensitivity is emotional dysregulation. This was probably one of the most liberating things to learn about when I received my ADHD/VAST diagnosis at age 34. I had spent my entire life wondering why I wasn't able to control my emotions like "everyone else" around me, or so it seemed. As a child I was quick to tear up whenever I felt slighted or hurt, and no one ever seemed as excited as I felt for things like birthdays and Christmas.

Feedback, from report cards to my first job evaluations felt like torture, even when they were mostly positive. No matter what I did I always seemed to need days if not weeks to recover from any slight or perceived slight from friends, family, or coworkers. This resulted in my hearing time and time again that I needed to "grow a thicker skin," and to let things "roll off my back." However, there were never any instructions on HOW to do that, I was just told that I needed to do so. This set me up for thinking that I was somehow obviously defective as a human. What other conclusion could I come to given that I could never seem to figure out how to follow through on this "grow a thicker skin" advice?

Upon entering ministry and the professional world, this cycle of events did not improve. I was now being told time and time again that I was to be the "non-anxious presence," in situations from board meetings to hospital rooms. Again, this felt laughable as I did not yet know or understand that my experience of emotional dysregulation was simply a trait of VAST and the way my brain is wired. In fact, it is precisely what allows me to be as empathetic and compassionate as I am as a clergyperson because it allows me to more easily slip into someone else's shoes.

Rather than encouraging clergy to be the "non-anxious presence," changing the language to "less anxious" would be helpful on the part of churches and church leadership. Simply changing the culture that can all too often place clergy on pedestals and instead allowing us to be fully human would provide a greater sense of psychological security for us. As Pastor Louise says, "I think so much of it just comes down to awareness and then normalizing and supporting."[14]

Another thing to consider for churches and church leadership is to assess your church's culture around flexibility. Are you a congregation that needs everything to happen at a certain time without much room for change? Often VAST and other neurodiverse clergy experience what I have come to call "Bad Brain Days." These are days where I either am having an immense amount of trouble focusing, or am feeling inexplicably "off," for reasons I often cannot articulate. Having the understanding from the congregation and normalizing the postponing or rescheduling of meetings on "Bad Brain Days," would be such a gift.

In the instances where cancelling, rescheduling, or postponing simply aren't feasible, as these cases do happen, and your VAST or otherwise neurodivergent clergyperson has to "rally" to get through the event, meeting, or day of ministry, the flexibility to allow her to modify her schedule the next day or over the next week would be a small miracle.

Giving pastors the time they need to re-regulate their systems after intense periods of work and ministry would be an incredible gift. While it is nearly impossible to see, especially if your clergyperson has spent a lifetime of "masking" and adapting to fit in, your VAST clergyperson is likely in need of true and deep rest on a more frequent basis to stay healthy in all forms.

Hyperfocus

Unlike many of the other traits that can certainly feel more like a disability than a superpower, hyperfocus has more often been described by the participants in this study as something that is generally a benefit in their ministerial lives. Hyperfocus comes and goes and is unfortunately unpredictable, but when we find ourselves in that near-perfect "flow state," our one main request is not to interrupt it.

When we're allowed to truly immerse ourselves in the project at

---

14. Louise, "008.Louise."

hand, especially if it is one that we are passionate about or that has captivated our interest and is scratching that need for dopamine, that's when magic can happen. However, if that focus is broken, it can take us a long time to get it back, if we ever do. Pastor Ruby shares the double-edged sword of this trait, "When I hyperfocus on sermon preparation, I can create something truly meaningful, but I have to be careful about how long I stay in that zone."[15]

One of the best ideas I ever experienced in an office environment was the creation of red, yellow, and green stop light-colored signs. Each person in the office received a set, and the signs were attached to magnets so they could be hung on the metal shelving above workstations or on the metal doorframes of those who had private offices. The green signs meant, "Come on in, I'm free to talk," the yellow signs meant, "Please give me a minute," and the red signs meant, "Do Not Disturb." It was an easy way to let our colleagues know if we were working on something that we needed to concentrate fully on or if we were on a phone call or meeting, and when we were open to interruption. This system would be an easy and cost-effective way to implement a simple strategy for your VAST clergywoman to communicate with others when she is hyperfocused and realizes it would be helpful to avoid having her window of focus interrupted.

Timeblindness

To repeat, the answers from participants regarding timeblindness are written responses as a follow up to their initial interviews. I had originally overlooked including this incredibly prevalent trait into the interview questionnaire. It is fortuitous that one of the participants caught this oversight and brought it to my attention while there was still enough time for me to reach out to the participants and inquire about how this trait affects their ministries. I also asked for their insight and vision as to how churches and church leaders could better support them in managing this trait and succeeding in ministry.

One of the easiest things church leadership boards, church admin

---

15. Ruby, "001.Ruby."

assistants, and others could implement would be to simply give their clergy person "…clear, honest, true deadlines for everything."[16] While many people probably assume it is more graceful and kind to say things like, "Just get it to me whenever," this is nearly always a death sentence for whatever it is they need from their VAST clergyperson— the monthly church newsletter article, the budget report, the plan for Vacation Bible School, anything. This is because VAST brains have only two settings, "NOW" and "NOT NOW."

Deadlines help us "see time," and when we can place deadlines on our calendars, on sticky notes, and in our reminder apps, it exponentially increases the likelihood that we will follow through on the task at hand and return the items being requested by the time they are needed to avoid holding the other person up from completing their own work.

Timeblindness and its effects on our lives is one of the most anxiety and stress inducing traits that we contend with as VAST clergywomen. For so many cultures we find ourselves working in, being on time seems to be a major criterion for deciding whether someone is responsible, caring, competent, and invested in their job. As someone whose anxiety kept her on time or exceedingly early for things for most of her life, let me tell you it was an abrupt switch when my anxiety was finally controlled, and the VAST timeblindness became more noticeable. Instead of running early for meetings, for work, for lunch with friends, I was consistently five or more minutes late.

Whether it is showing up for in person events or ensuring we turn needed documents and reports in on time, timeblindness is one of our biggest challenges. Being late can launch us into our shame, our anxiety, and sometimes even our depression spirals. Pastor Louise shares how helpful features such as the Gmail "nudge" feature have become for her,

> I mean, one thing's super simple, but the way we even do reminders in an email. I always have the fear that I will miss data and miss things. So, I'm like hypervigilant about following every and all my systems and everything right, but it would be

---

16. Fiona, "003.Fiona."

lovely if there was often a little more grace around deadlines and some gentle reminders. I think that for a lot of people that I talk with that's just that executive function of the administrative part of the work. For administrators to really be gentle and kind in that, in their tone would just be beautiful. Because I have judged ADHD people who can't get on a deadline and can't get with it. I'm like, 'You're being lazy.' I'm like, 'Louise, you know. That is not what's happening.'[17]

As Pastor Louise states, even as clergy and people who contend with this trait ourselves, it is often one of the ones that we find ourselves judging the most often in others. It is past time for a cultural shift, especially in Western cultures, to see time differently.

Timeblindness is truly, I believe, a profound spiritual gift of your VAST clergy—we naturally live more in *Kairos* or "God's Time" than in *Kronos* or human time. Why not finally acknowledge this as a gift of the Holy Spirit that has been given to your church? Let your VAST clergywoman help you live in God's time more consistently and see what incredible things follow.

> It is past time for a cultural shift, especially in Western cultures, to see time differently.

Divergent Thinking

Finally, the unparalleled and most amazing gift your VAST clergywoman has is her supernatural ability to think outside the metaphorical box. Oftentimes churches will articulate a desire for change, claiming they long for their church to grow and that they are willing to try new things. However, VAST clergywomen are more consistently met with the age old, "But we've never done it that way before," when they offer new and innovative ideas for consideration. It can be disheartening and ruffle that rejection sensitivity when our ideas are consistently shot down. And for some of us, the cognitive dissonance of being told time and time again that the church wants to and is

---

17. Louise, "008.Louise."

willing to change but being met with perpetual resistance is unbearable. It is this loop that will quickly push us closer and closer to the edge of wanting to walk away from ministry entirely.

Pastor Marley advises churches to, 'Just allow it. Go with it. Be okay with the chaos. Allow space for imagination… I think, allowing space for the imagination of the Holy Spirit, because I think so much of what we… we as ADHD people do is not just form, like, I think 'my' idea. They're my ideas. But it's also through the leaning into… into Spirit and into where we're being… we're being led. Like, try new things…"[18]

Speaking only for myself, I know it can feel nearly impossible to articulate to my congregation or ministry setting that the new or creative idea I am pitching to them is one that I believe is coming from God. Even for pastors, it can feel a little woo-woo to say that we heard something from God or the Holy Spirit. At worst, it can even feel manipulative, as who is going to be able to prove, really, whether the idea is yours or divinely inspired? This is an incredibly narrow line to try and traverse as a pastor. Once again, the best advice we can offer is to encourage and train your churches to be as flexible as possible. Only when churches are willing to try new things and follow the creativity of their VAST clergyperson will they know what is possible.

For denominational leaders a good, hard, honest look at our ordination policies, procedures and practices is needed. As Pastor Nicole laments, "Saying you want to do anything differently is not the way to get ordained."[19] For many VAST clergy it is precisely our creative thinking and the spiritual giftedness of that which led us to discern our calls to ministry in the first place. We hear the cries of the church that they want to survive, thrive, grow and be more relevant in the world today. And it is our heart's desire to help them obtain those goals through creativity and innovation.

Unfortunately, too many of us have learned the hard way that there are unspoken rules in our current systems and have surmised that if we do not answer ordination questions a certain way, or appear to fit

18. Marley, "007.Marley."
19. Nicole, "005.Nicole."

Recommendations for supporting neurodivergent clergywomen

in a certain type of model, then our chances at getting ordained in our tradition of choice becomes slimmer and slimmer. Many of us feel a tension between staying true to ourselves and maintaining our integrity as opposed to saying the "right thing," simply to pass through the arduous process of ordination. Once again, I fear that we are perpetuating systems and patterns that lead to little more than burning competent, qualified, and called clergy out before they even receive their first pastoral assignments.

> Instead of assigning or installing your VAST clergywomen to those churches that you know may talk a good game about wanting to change but truly aren't ready, why not help guide them to the churches that are most likely to benefit from their unique giftedness?

The more open and flexible both local churches and regional adjudicatory bodies can become, the more possibilities lie ahead for everyone. And for those who can see the broader lay of the land such as bishops and regional ministers, it is advised to keep in mind the gifts and graces of your neurodiverse clergywomen. Instead of assigning or installing your VAST clergywomen to those churches that you know may talk a good game about wanting to change but truly aren't ready, why not help guide them to the churches that are most likely to benefit from their unique giftedness? The time to consider a change in how we deploy VAST clergywomen is now.

In conclusion, there are some key things to do as church and denominational leaders if you want to increase support for your VAST and otherwise neurodivergent clergy. These include trying things differently, being flexible, assuming the best intent, respecting healthy boundaries instituted by your clergyperson, extending grace and approaching one another with curiosity and grace rather than judgement and assumptions. It will require investing time and energy to educate ourselves about VAST and neurodiversity in general so the weight of helping you understand does not fall upon the neurodiverse community. And of course, it will require returning to the basics and showing each other simple respect.

Whether it's through video training, workshops, continuing education events, compiling expert panels or other means, the time and investment put into training church boards and denominational leaders on how to best support VAST and neurodiverse clergy will reap net benefits across the board for generations.

Conclusion

As a pastor myself, it is a rare treat when I get to worship with my own family. Perhaps this is why a specific children's moment at my parents' church remains with me as one of the most powerful and memorable children's moments I can remember ever having witnessed. That Sunday, I was worshipping with my niece in the pews at "Grandma & Papa's church," and was delighted when she bounded up the aisle to sit at the feet of the children's ministry director.

That Sunday, the children were given Möbius strips as a take-home object lesson. Möbius strips are, according to Scientific American, "an artist's reverie and a mathematician's feat."[1] By giving a half twist to a long rectangular piece of paper and attaching the two ends, a shape is created that only has one side. As you trace your finger along the strip you can continue in endless loops. There is no top and no bottom, no inside nor outside. It is truly an entrancing experience and immediately captured the attention of the children (and adults, too!).

"Every ending is a beginning, and every beginning is an ending," said the woman at the front as she expertly discussed deep theological truths with the children in a way that, at least some of the older ones, might be able to grasp as they held the Möbius strips in their hand. It is this deep theological truth that has helped sustain me through this work and gives me hope as I look toward the future for VAST and neurodiverse clergywomen and the church.

For many of us, receiving our ADHD/VAST diagnoses was both a beginning and an ending. It was the beginning of having to re-learn who we are and why our brains work the way they do. It is, hopefully, the end of living in an endless and vicious cycle of shame and the

---

1. Alagappan, "The Timeless Journey of the Möbius Strip."

beginning of extending to ourselves more grace and understanding than we've ever been able to muster before.

Likewise, my hope and prayer are that this project will be the beginning of a new conversation within the church, especially among church leaders. I hope that this work will inspire those in positions of leadership to learn more about not only VAST, but the many and varied ways that our brains can be different from one another. I hope for the end of expecting all pastors to be exactly alike. I pray it is the beginning of helping churches, church leadership, and VAST clergy ourselves to see our neurodiversity not only as a physiological and psychological reality, but also as a *spiritual gift*.

How beautiful would it be to be able to witness, in our lifetimes, the end of stigma and misunderstanding and the beginning of affirmation and celebration for the varied and diverse ways in which God has created us and called some of us into ministry not despite, but *because of* the way our brains are beautifully and differently wired?

Of course, just as we—clergy, churches, and church leadership alike —begin to make progress here, something else will arise. I haven't even mentioned in this work the research beginning to emerge regarding how hormone fluctuations both monthly and at different life stages for women and uterus-owning persons such as perimenopause and menopause can affect and change how VAST presents. Or the reactions changing hormone levels can have with different medications, tampering with their effectiveness. It's possible that just as a VAST clergyperson and their church find a smooth-sailing rhythm, something will change or shift that will feel like one or both parties are taking several steps backward rather than forward.

It is my prayer, in these cases, that the most basic and foundational of strategies for understanding, support, and collaboration we have discussed here for churches and church leadership will be of help. That, with education and heightened understanding of VAST and other neurodiversity conditions, leaders will first and foremost turn to curiosity and empathy, rather than assumptions and confusion. That they will extend grace and a listening ear to clergy who may seem to be struggling out of the blue. And that clergy may feel empowered to be curious about their own experiences. That they will find the support and allyship of their congregations and denominational leadership to explore together the shifts and changing tides of the seasons of life and ministry and VAST all together.

There is no doubt that the decades of misunderstanding and neglect of how VAST affects girls and women have had a negative effect on those of us who have been diagnosed as adults. While we often managed to find our own coping strategies, learned to mirror our peers so we could "mask" our traits in order to better fit in, and were by and large successful in school and our academic journeys, the fact that 80% of the interview participants and myself all report poor self-esteem and battling negative self-perception is telling. Before we even enter the pastorate, a vocation known for its rigor and penchant for subjecting those who enter it to elevated levels of... commentary... from what and how we preach to the way we lead meetings to what we wear and how our hair is styled, we are already half convinced that we aren't worthy to lead.

In addition to the practical strategies and supports that have been outlined, such as breaking up longer denominational meetings and ensuring that congregations are well trained in *writing shit down* for their clergyperson on the regular, the most helpful changes churches can make are simply to flex their ability to learn. To try to understand, and to remain flexible and open to trying new or at least different ways of operating and working with their VAST clergyperson. In doing so, I truly believe that our churches and communities will be blown away by the tremendous amount of joy, vision, and energy that the Spirit will let loose as their spiritually gifted, differently wired, completely unique clergywomen are allowed to lean in and follow the guiding of that same Spirit into a new and exciting future for the church and the world.

~

Katharine L. Steele

May God the nursing Mother[2] open the eyes of the church to the shimmering beauty of and unique perspectives provided by our "neuro-sparkly" clergywomen.

May Jesus the Redeemer free the minds, hearts, and spirits of neurodiverse clergywomen everywhere to see themselves as the gifted children of God they are.

And may the Creative Spirit and Wisdom of God lead us forth into a new beginning of deeper understanding, creative cooperation, and joyful acceptance all.

For the transformation of the world hangs in the balance.

Amen.

---

2. Wil Gafney

Bibliography

Alagappan, Serena. "The Timeless Journey of the Möbius Strip." *Scientific American*, January 16, 2021. scientificamerican.com/article/the-timeless-journey-of-the-moebius-strip.

Brook. 2024. Interview by Katharine L. Steele. *Faith, Health & Social Equity*.

Collier, Elizabeth J. 1999. "United Methodist Clergywomen Retention Study." Anna Howard Shaw Center. 2024. https://www.bu.edu/shaw/publications/the-clergy-womens-retention-study/united-methodist-clergywomens-retention-study-3/.

Crawford, Nicole. "ADHD: A Women's Issue." *Monitor* 34, no. 2 (February 2003). apa.org/monitor/feb03/adhd.

Eiesland, Nancy L. 1994. *The Disabled God: Toward a Liberatory Theology of Disability*. Nashville, TN: Abingdon.

Elizabeth. 024. Interview by Katharine L. Steele. *Faith, Health & Social Equity*.

Evans, Selma. 2023. *Women with Adhd; Effective Strategies to Stay Organized, Manage Your Emotions, Your Finances and Succeed in Life*.

Faulkner, Noelle. 2020. "The Lost Girls: 'Chaotic and Curious, Women with Adhd All Have Missed Red Flags That Haunt Us'." 2021. https://getpocket.com/explore/item/the-lost-girls-chaotic-and-curious-women-with-adhd-all-have-missed-red-flags-that-haunt-us?fbclid=IwAR3GDYC1X2-5ElNH-IJC1GWf5sILnaaXTYZP91Kos7IQK78IjjNzPmy_f-c.

Fiona. 2024. Interview by Katharine L. Steele. *Faith, Health & Social Equity*.

Gloria. 2024. Interview by Katharine L. Steele. *Faith, Health & Social Equity*.

Hallowell, Edward. *ADHD Explained*. Unabridged. DK, 2023.

Hallowell, Edward M. 2006. *Delivered from Distraction: Getting the Most out of Life with Attention Deficit Disorder*. New York: Ballantine Books.

Hallowell, Edward M. *Driven to Distraction at Work: How to Focus and Be More Productive*, edited by Harvard Business Review Press. Boston, Massachusetts. 2015.

Hallowell, Edward M., and John J. Ratey. 1995. *Driven to Distraction: Recognizing and Coping with Attention Deficit Disorder from Childhood through Adulthood*. New York: Simon & Schuster.

Hallowell, Edward M., 2013. *Answers to Distraction*: Anchor.

Hallowell, Ned. 2011. *Shine*, edited by Harvard Business Press. Boston, MA: Harvard Business Press.

Hallowell, Ned, and John Ratey. 2021. *Adhd 2.0: New Science and Essential Strategies for Thriving with Distraction- from Childhood through Adulthood*. New York: Ballantine Books.

Hill, Linda. 2022. *Women with Adhd*: Peak Publish LLC.

Horan, Lynn. "Feminized Servanthood, Gendered Scapegoating, and the Disappearance of Gen-X/Millennial Protestant Clergy Women." Yellow Springs, OH, 2024. https://aura.antioch.edu/etds/1063.

"How Many Quit? Estimating the Clergy Attrition Rate." Transition Into Ministry. Lilly

Bibliography

Endowment, 2025. into-action.net/research/many-quit-estimating-clergy-attrition-rate/.

Kelly, Kate, and Peggy Ramundo. 1998. *The Added Dimension: Celebrating the Opportunities, Rewards and Challenges of the Add Experience*. New York: Simon & Schuster.

Kelly, Kate, and Peggy Ramundo. 2006. *You Mean I'm Not Lazy, Stupid or Crazy?!: The Classic Self-Help Book for Adults with Attention Deficit Disorder*. London: Simon & Schuster.

Levrini, Abigail L. 2023. *Succeeding with Adult Adhd*, edited by American Psychological Association: American Psychological Association.

Louise. 2024. Interview by Katharine L. Steele. *Faith, Health & Social Equity*.

Marley. 2024. Interview by Katharine L. Steele. *Faith, Health & Social Equity*.

Matlen, Terry. 2014. *The Queen of Distraction*: New Harbinger Publications.

McCabe, Jessica. "How to Adhd." YouTube channel.

McCabe, Jessica. 2024. *How to Adhd*: Souvenir Press.

Michelle. 2024. Interview by Katharine L. Steele. *Faith, Health & Social Equity*.

Nicole. 2024. Interview by Katharine L. Steele. *Faith, Health & Social Equity*.

"Pastors Share Top Reasons They've Considered Quitting Ministry in the Past Year." 2022. Barna Group. Accessed September 12, 2023. Form of Item.

Pink, Richard, and Roxanne Emery. 2023. *Dirty Laundry*: Ten Speed Press.

Rosier, Tamara. 2021. *Your Brain's Not Broken: Strategies for Navigating Your Emotions and Life with Adhd*. Grand Rapids, Michigan: Rivell, A Division of Baker Publishing Group.

Ruby. 2024. Interview by Katharine L. Steele. *Faith, Health & Social Equity*.

Proeschold-Bell, R.J., and S. LeGrand. "High Rates of Obesity and Chronic Disease among United Methodist Clergy." *Obesity* 18, no. 9 (2010): 1867—70. https://doi.org/10.1038/oby.2010.102.

Reuter, Reuter. "The Three Marys." Washington D.C., 2008.

Sans, Leo. 2024. "Adhd-Like Traits Could Offer Humans an Advantage in Foraging, Study Suggests." *The Washington Post* (February 22, 2024). Accessed February 22, 2024.

"Seriously?" Women in Ministry Video. North Carolina, 2018. youtube.com/watch?v=bTcaAkG86QQ.

Skoglund, LB. 2023. *Adhd Girls to Women: Getting on the Radar*. Philadelphia, PA: Jessica Kingsley Publishers.

Solden, Sari, Michelle Frank, and Ellen Littman. 2019. *A Radical Guide for Women with Adhd: Embrace Neurodiversity, Live Boldly, and Breakthrough Barriers*. Ann Arbor, MI: Oakland New Harbinger Publications.

Sophia. 2024. Interview by Katharine L. Steele. *Faith, Health & Social Equity*.

Ter Beek, LS, MN Bohmer, ME Wittekoek, and JJS Kooij. 2023. "Lifetime Adhd Symptoms Highly Prevalent in Women with Cardiovascular Complaints. A Cross-Sectional Study." *Women's Mental Health*.

Tracy, Otsuka. *ADHD For Smart Ass Women*. Unabridged. Harper Audio, 2023.

WH, Canu, Cave MJ, and Nelson JM. 2024. "Stigma Related to Observable Symptoms, but Not Stimulant Medication Use, in Young Women with Adhd." *Journal of Attention Disorders*.

"Women and Girls." 2023. CHADD. Accessed September 12, 2023.